Terraform for Google Cloud Essential Guide

Learn how to provision infrastructure in Google Cloud securely and efficiently

Bernd Nordhausen

BIRMINGHAM—MUMBAI

Terraform for Google Cloud Essential Guide

Group Product Manager: Rahul Nair
Publishing Product Manager: Niranjan Naikwadi
Content Development Editor: Sujata Tripathi
Technical Editor: Nithik Cheruvakodan
Copy Editor: Safis Editing
Project Coordinator: Sean Lobo
Proofreader: Safis Editing
Indexer: Tejal Daruwale Soni
Production Designer: Aparna Bhagat
Senior Marketing Coordinator: Nimisha Dua
Marketing Coordinator: Gaurav Christian

First published: January 2023

Production reference: 1161222

Published by Packt Publishing Ltd.
Livery Place
35 Livery Street
Birmingham
B3 2PB, UK.

ISBN 978-1-80461-962-9

www.packt.com

Contributors

About the author

Bernd Nordhausen is an independent cloud consultant and Google Cloud trainer. He is a seasoned cloud architect with over 25 years of experience working with industry leaders such as Intel and Accenture. He holds over a dozen cloud certifications from all three major cloud service providers.

Bernd was previously the technical lead for the Google Cloud practice at Accenture Southeast Asia. In that role, he developed and implemented several large-scale deployments on Google Cloud using Terraform.

In a different century, Bernd received his B.Sc. in mathematics from the University of Alabama, and his M.Sc. and Ph.D. in computer science from the University of California, Irvine. When his head is not in the cloud, Bernd is an aspiring woodworker and trail runner. He also has a website where he talks more about his work, expertise, services and life at `https://www.nordhausenconsulting.com/`

I'd like to thank Packt for reaching out and encouraging me to write this book, and then for the great people they brought in to help. I particularly want to thank Radek Simko for his excellent feedback. His input made this book what it is.

About the reviewer

Radek Simko is a senior software engineer at HashiCorp. He has been involved in various parts of the Terraform ecosystem for the last 5 years. He has contributed to maintaining the AWS provider, created the official Kubernetes provider, and bootstrapped the initial decoupled version of the plugin SDK. Since early 2020, he has been focusing on improving support for Terraform in editors via a dedicated language server. Prior to HashiCorp, he worked at Time Inc. for over 3 years, where he pioneered Terraform and proposed a number of bug fixes and features externally as an open-source contributor. Radek was born and raised in the Czech Republic, but he calls the UK his second home and enjoys traveling in his free time.

Table of Contents

3

Writing Efficient Terraform Code   41

4

Writing Reusable Code Using Modules   57

5

Managing Environments   71

Part 2: Completing the Picture: Provisioning Infrastructure on Google Cloud

6

7

8

Part 3: Wrapping It Up: Integrating Terraform with Google Cloud

9

Preface

Google Cloud has adopted Terraform as the standard **Infrastructure-as-Code (IaC)** tool. Thus, a good understanding of Terraform is essential for any cloud architect and engineer working on Google Cloud. Yet no specific resources are available that focus on how to use Terraform on Google Cloud.

This book is the first book that teaches the reader about Terraform specifically for Google Cloud. We will take you on a journey from the basic concepts to deploying complex architectures using Terraform. Using easy-to-understand code examples, we will show you how to authenticate Terraform in Google Cloud, teach you all the essential concepts of the Terraform language as applied to Google Cloud, and deploy complete working architectures at the push of a button. We will also show you how to improve your Terraform workflow using Google Cloud-native and third-party tools.

By the end of this book, you will have gained a thorough understanding of Terraform and how to use it on Google Cloud. You will have learned how to develop effective Terraform code, build reusable modules, and utilize public domain Terraform modules to deploy on Google Cloud faster and more securely.

Who this book is for

If you are working in Google Cloud and want to become more efficient in provisioning and managing Google Cloud infrastructure, this book is for you. We teach you the rationale of IaC and guide you on how to use Terraform as the IaC tool for Google Cloud. We will take you on a journey from provisioning a virtual machine using a single file to deploying multi-tiered architecture in different environments at the proverbial push of a button.

What this book covers

Chapter 1, Getting Started with Terraform on Google Cloud, introduces the concept of IaC before provisioning virtual machines using four methods of authenticating Terraform in Google Cloud.

Chapter 2, Exploring Terraform, details how Terraform uses state information to decide what actions to take. It also explains the use of meta-arguments, which enable you to write effective Terraform code.

Chapter 3, Writing Efficient Terraform Code, introduces specific Terraform constructs to help you develop efficient Terraform code and explains how to expose Terraform state information.

Chapter 4, Writing Reusable Code Using Modules, explains how to develop Terraform Modules to reuse and share Terraform code.

Chapter 5, *Managing Environments*, compares the two primary methods to manage multiple environments using the same Terraform code base.

Chapter 6, *Deploying a Traditional Three-Tier Architecture*, uses the concepts introduced so far to build a complete three-tier architecture.

Chapter 7, *Deploying a Cloud-Native Architecture Using Cloud Run*, continues to apply the concepts learned to deploy a cloud-native, completely serverless architecture.

Chapter 8, *Deploying GKE Using Public Modules*, describes how to use two of the most common Public Modules to deploy a development and production GKE cluster using only differing variable assignments.

Chapter 9, *Developing Terraform Code Efficiently*, introduces four of the most common tools to improve your Terraform workflow.

Chapter 10, *Google Cloud Integration*, shows how to use Cloud Build to create a CI/CD pipeline for Terraform and introduces a unique Google Cloud feature for importing existing cloud resources into the realm of Terraform.

To get the most out of this book

You should have a basic knowledge of Google Cloud, including how to provision Google cloud resources using the web console and the Google Cloud command-line interface, `gcloud`. We use Ubuntu and the Bash shell but Terraform and `gcloud` work equally well on macOS using `zsh` and on Windows using `PowerShell`.

Download the example code files

You can download the example code files for this book from GitHub at `https://github.com/PacktPublishing/Terraform-for-Google-Cloud-Essential-Guide`. If there's an update to the code, it will be updated in the GitHub repository.

We also have other code bundles from our rich catalog of books and videos available at `https://github.com/PacktPublishing/`. Check them out!

Download the color images

We also provide a PDF file that has color images of the screenshots and diagrams used in this book. You can download it here: `https://packt.link/yzxje`.

Conventions used

There are a number of text conventions used throughout this book.

Code in text: Indicates code words in text, database table names, folder names, filenames, file extensions, pathnames, dummy URLs, user input, and Twitter handles. Here is an example: "By convention, we have three files: main.tf, which contains the main code, variables.tf, which defines the variables that need to be passed to the module, and outputs.tf, which contains the information passed back to the calling module."

A block of code is set as follows:

```
output "public_ip_address" {
  value = var.static_ip ? google_compute_instance.this.network_
interface.0.access_config.0.nat_ip : null
}
output "private_ip_address" {
  value = google_compute_instance.this.network_
interface.0.network_ip
}
output "self_link" {
  value = google_compute_instance.this.self_link
}
```

When we wish to draw your attention to a particular part of a code block, the relevant lines or items are set in bold:

```
module "deny_ssh_ingress" {
  source        = "terraform-google-modules/network/google//
modules/firewall-rules"
  version       = "5.2.0"
  project_id    = var.project_id
  network_name = module.network.network_name
```

Any command-line input or output is written as follows:

```
$ terraform init
$ terraform apply
$ terraform state list
```

Bold: Indicates a new term, an important word, or words that you see onscreen. For instance, words in menus or dialog boxes appear in **bold**. Here is an example: "Using **Web Console**, go to **Cloud Overview | Activity**, and look at the…"

> Tips or important notes
> Appear like this.

Get in touch

Feedback from our readers is always welcome.

General feedback: If you have questions about any aspect of this book, email us at customercare@ packtpub.com and mention the book title in the subject of your message.

Errata: Although we have taken every care to ensure the accuracy of our content, mistakes do happen. If you have found a mistake in this book, we would be grateful if you would report this to us. Please visit www.packtpub.com/support/errata and fill in the form.

Piracy: If you come across any illegal copies of our works in any form on the internet, we would be grateful if you would provide us with the location address or website name. Please contact us at copyright@packt.com with a link to the material.

If you are interested in becoming an author: If there is a topic that you have expertise in and you are interested in either writing or contributing to a book, please visit authors.packtpub.com.

Share Your Thoughts

Once you've read *Terraform for Google Cloud Essential Guide*, we'd love to hear your thoughts! Scan the QR code below to go straight to the Amazon review page for this book and share your feedback.

https://packt.link/r/1804619620

Your review is important to us and the tech community and will help us make sure we're delivering excellent quality content.

Download a free PDF copy of this book

Thanks for purchasing this book!

Do you like to read on the go but are unable to carry your print books everywhere? Is your eBook purchase not compatible with the device of your choice?

Don't worry, now with every Packt book you get a DRM-free PDF version of that book at no cost.

Read anywhere, any place, on any device. Search, copy, and paste code from your favorite technical books directly into your application.

The perks don't stop there, you can get exclusive access to discounts, newsletters, and great free content in your inbox daily

Follow these simple steps to get the benefits:

1. Scan the QR code or visit the link below

https://packt.link/free-ebook/9781804619629

2. Submit your proof of purchase
3. That's it! We'll send your free PDF and other benefits to your email directly

Part 1: Getting Started: Learning the Fundamentals

The first part covers the fundamentals of Terraform for Google Cloud. We start with an overview of Infrastructure as Code and Terraform, then show four methods to authenticate Terraform with Google Cloud. We introduce the Terraform workflow and go in-depth into the Terraform state file, which is essential to understand how Terraform operates. *Chapter 3* introduces some of the unique concepts of the Terraform language that help to write Terraform code. *Chapter 4* introduces Terraform modules so you can reuse and share Terraform code and utilize public Terraform modules. There are two main methods of managing multiple environments such as development, testing, and production in Terraform. *Chapter 5* details both of them and discusses the pros and cons of each approach.

Throughout *Part 1*, we use simple but realistic code examples to focus on the language concepts. After reading *Part 1*, you will have a thorough understanding of the Terraform language and its inner workings, so you can build complex deployments in Google Cloud using Terraform.

This part of the book comprises the following chapters:

- *Chapter 1, Getting Started with Terraform on Google Cloud*
- *Chapter 2, Exploring Terraform*
- *Chapter 3, Writing Efficient Terraform Code*
- *Chapter 4, Writing Reusable Code Using Modules*
- *Chapter 5, Managing Environments*

1
Getting Started with Terraform on Google Cloud

Let us start with a brief introduction to DevOps and the central role of **Infrastructure as Code (IaC)** in this emerging software development practice. Then, we will discuss why Terraform has emerged as the de facto IaC tool and why knowing Terraform is essential for any aspiring cloud engineer and cloud architect. After that, you will learn how to use Terraform to provision resources in Google Cloud.

Thus, by the end of the chapter, you will better understand why you should use Terraform to provision cloud infrastructure. You'll also have learned how to authenticate Terraform and provision your first Google Cloud resources using Terraform.

In this chapter, we are going to cover the following main topics:

- The rise of DevOps
- Running Terraform in Google Cloud Shell
- Running Terraform in your local environment
- Parameterizing Terraform
- Comparing authentication methods

Technical requirements

This chapter and the remainder of this book require you to have a Google Cloud account. You can use an existing Google Cloud project, but we recommend creating a new clean project for you to follow along. You should also have the Google Cloud **command-line interface (CLI)** installed on your local PC and be familiar with basic `gcloud` commands. Please see `https://cloud.google.com/sdk/docs/install` for detailed instructions on how to download the CLI.

Of course, we are using Terraform. Terraform is available on all common operating systems and is easy to install. You can download the version for your operating system at `https://www.terraform.io/downloads`. HashiCorp is constantly improving the tool by providing updates and upgrades. For the writing of this book, we are using v1.3.3. The code should work with any version greater than v.1.3.0. However, we suggest you download this particular version if you run into any issues.

The source code for this chapter and all other chapters is available at `https://github.com/PacktPublishing/Terraform-for-Google-Cloud-Essential-Guide`.

We recommend that you download the code, enabling you to follow along. We organized the code into analogous chapters and sections and indicated the appropriate subdirectories.

The rise of DevOps

The rise of cloud computing since mid-2000 has been spectacular. Hardly a month goes by without the three hyperscalers (**Amazon Web Services** (**AWS**), Azure, and Google Cloud) announcing the opening of a new data center region. Cloud computing—in particular, public cloud—offers an incredible array of technologies at a nearly infinite scale. This has led to a new way of deploying and operating IT. DevOps combines two areas that were traditionally distinct phases in software development—development and operations. DevOps aims to deliver software at a much faster pace than the traditional Waterfall model was able to. By combining historically distinct phases and teams, DevOps methodology can deliver software much more rapidly and with higher quality than traditional software methodology.

One key aspect of DevOps is automation. Combining several separate tools into a pipeline, we can deliver software from development to production with minimal human intervention. This concept of **continuous integration and continuous delivery**, usually referred to as **CI/CD**, integrates managing source code, provisioning the IT infrastructure, compiling (if necessary), packaging, testing, and deploying into a pipeline. A CI/CD pipeline requires automation at every step to execute efficiently.

Infrastructure as Code

Automating the provisioning of the IT infrastructure is a key component of a CI/CD pipeline and is known as IaC. In traditional on-prem computing, servers and networking infrastructure provision was a long-drawn and manual process. It started with ordering IT hardware, the physical setup of the hardware, and configuration, such as installing the operating system and configuring the network infrastructure. This process would often take weeks or months. Virtualization somewhat helped the process, but the provisioning of the infrastructure would generally still fall onto a separate team before developers could start deploying the fruit of their labor into a test environment, much less a production one.

The rise of cloud computing shortened this process from months to days and even hours. Infrastructure can now be provisioned through a **graphical user interface (GUI)** known as the web console. Initially, this was a straightforward process as the number of services and configuration options were manageable. However, as more services became available and the configuration options increased exponentially, provisioning networks, servers, databases, and other managed services became tedious and error-prone.

A key objective in DevOps is to have essentially identical environments. That is, the development, test, and production environments should be the same except for some minor configuration changes; for example, the database in development and production should be identical except for the number of CPUs and the size of memory.

However, configuring complex environments using the web console is tedious and error prone. Using what is sometimes derided as **ClickOps**, the provisioning of even a medium-complex environment requires hundreds, if not thousands, of user interactions or clicks.

Using a CLI can help with configuring multiple environments. One can develop scripts that combine multiple CLI commands into a single executable. However, managing and making changes is next to impossible using a CLI.

Enter IaC. IaC is the provisioning of infrastructure using code rather than a web console or a CLI. For example, you can write code to achieve the same step instead of using the web console and going through several manual steps to provision a server. For example, the `main.tf` file featured in this chapter shows the configuration of a server with the Debian operating system. The server, called `cloudshell`, is an `e2-micro` instance placed in the `us-central1-a` region.

Once you have the code, you can reuse it repeatedly. That is, you can deploy many servers with minimal or no change. Since, it is regular code, you can use version control and source code revision systems to manage your code. This facilitates effective teamwork.

Furthermore, IaC can be integrated into a CI/CD pipeline, including testing and validation. That is, you can validate and test the provisioning of servers before they are deployed. Thus, you can provision complex infrastructure involving hundreds of servers, complex networking, and multiple services within minutes rather than days or weeks. Ultimately, this makes the software development release process faster and more secure, which is precisely the objective of DevOps.

A CI/CD pipeline includes many steps besides IaC. One of the steps is configuration management, which includes configuring servers such as installing updates, libraries, and code. Ansible, Puppet, and Chef are common configuration management tools. Some overlap exists between configuration management tools and IaC tools. Configuration management tools can provision some infrastructure, while IaC tools perform some configuration tasks. However, infrastructure provisioning and configuration management should generally be considered two separate steps better served by different tools.

Terraform

Terraform has become the most popular IaC tool in recent years. While each cloud platform has its proprietary IaC tool (AWS has **CloudFormation**, Azure has **Azure Resource Manager**, and Google Cloud has **Deployment Manager**), Terraform is unique in that it is platform agnostic. You can use Terraform to provision infrastructure in any cloud provider and for many other platforms such as vSphere and Google Workspace.

As you will see, Terraform is easy to learn and provides a straightforward workflow that can be easily incorporated into any CI tool. Terraform is open source and has developed an active community with its own ecosystem. Community members have developed tools that help you write Terraform code more effectively; we cover some of them in this book.

Running Terraform in Google Cloud Shell

> **Note**
>
> The code for this section is under chap01/cloudshell in the GitHub repo of this book.

The easiest way to run Terraform in Google Cloud is using Google **Cloud Shell**, which is a preconfigured development environment accessible through your browser. It comes pre-installed with the latest version of common utilities, including the latest version of Terraform. Furthermore, all authentication is already set up. So, let's give it a try.

> **Note**
>
> You can check the current version of Terraform using the terraform -version command.

If your project is new, and you have not provisioned a **virtual machine** (**VM**) (Compute Engine), run the following gcloud command to enable the compute API:

```
$ gcloud services enable compute.googleapis.com
```

Then place the following code in a file called main.tf. This is known as the Terraform configuration. Configurations are written in **HashiCorp Configuration Language** (**HCL**). HCL is human readable and is used by several HashiCorp tools.

> **Note**
>
> In this book, we will use the term *Terraform language* to refer to the language in which the configuration files are written.

This book aims to make you proficient in Terraform to write high-quality, reusable code to provision resources in Google Cloud efficiently and securely.

The file's actual name is arbitrary, but note that the .tf extension is mandatory. Terraform uses the .tf extension to identify Terraform configuration files.

main.tf

```
resource "google_compute_instance" "this" {
  name         = "cloudshell"
  machine_type = "e2-small"
  zone         = "us-central1-a"

  boot_disk {
    initialize_params {
      image = "debian-cloud/debian-11"
    }
  }

  network_interface {
    network = "default"
  }
}
```

Next, run the following two commands:

```
$ terraform init
$ terraform apply
```

Terraform will ask you where you want to perform these actions, so type in yes to approve.

Congratulations—you have now provisioned your first server using Terraform! Go to the web console and inspect the compute engine that Terraform has created.

As expected, Terraform created a Debian server named `cloudshell` of a machine type `e2-small` in the `default` network:

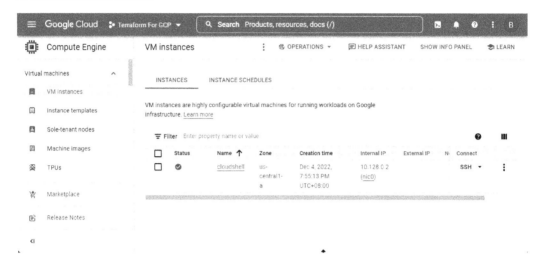

Figure 1.1 – Terraform-provisioned server in the web console

Let's have a more detailed look at how to write Terraform configurations and how Terraform operates.

Terraform language

As mentioned, the Terraform language is based on HCL. The most basic construct is a **block**, defined as a "*container for other content*" (`https://developer.hashicorp.com/terraform/language/syntax/configuration#blocks`). For example, the preceding code block is of the type `resource`. A resource block has two labels. The first label consists of the provider and resource name. For example, the resource label for a Google compute engine is `google_compute_instance`, whereas the label for an AWS E2 instance is `aws_instance`. The second label in a resource block is the ID, the name you give so that Terraform can uniquely identify each resource. Please note that no two resources can have the same name. So, if you want to provision two VMs, you define two resource blocks, each of type `google_compute_instance`, and each with a unique name.

The body of the block is nested within { }. Blocks can have nested blocks. In the preceding code example, there are two nested blocks, `boot_disk` (which in itself has a nested block called `initialize_params`) and `network_interface`.

While the syntax for Terraform is the same, each cloud provider has its unique **resources** and **data source** definitions. The Terraform documentation for Google Cloud is at `https://registry.terraform.io/providers/hashicorp/google/latest/docs`. You see that all resources and data sources start with the `google` keyword. In general, it is followed by the name of the equivalent `gcloud` command. Thus, the resource to create a compute instance is named `google_compute_instance`, whereas the resource to provision a SQL database instance is named `google_sql_database_instance`.

Looking at the documentation, you can see the current Google services that are currently supported. More are added as Google Cloud introduces new services. We recommend you bookmark the documentation as you have to refer to it frequently.

In the first part of this book, we use only a few Google Cloud resources as we want to concentrate on the language. We design complex architectures using additional Google Cloud services in the second part. But first, let's look at the steps involved in using Terraform.

Terraform workflow

A basic Terraform workflow consists of the following two steps:

1. `Init`
2. `Apply`

In this first step, `terraform init` initializes Terraform and downloads all the necessary configuration files. You see that after `init` is run, there is a hidden directory named `.terraform`. This directory is where Terraform stores various configuration files. You must run the initialization step every time you write a new configuration file. Don't worry; you can run this command multiple times, and you learn over time when you need to rerun it. If in doubt, run it again as it only takes a few seconds.

The second step, `terraform apply`, consists of two phases. First, Terraform creates an **execution plan**, then it executes this plan. The execution plan is an internal plan of the actions Terraform will perform and in which order. Terraform outputs this plan, including a summary of how many resources will be added, changed, and destroyed. You should *always* review this output carefully. Once you have confirmed that the plan does what you intended, you can confirm, and Terraform actually provisions the cloud resources.

You can also run the two phases explicitly by running `terraform plan`, saving the plan in a file, and then running `terraform apply` against that file, like so:

```
$ terraform plan --out=plan
$ terraform apply plan
```

This is often done in CI/CD pipelines, and we will return to it later.

One of the advantages of IaC is that you can quickly remove resources. This is not only useful during the development phase, as you can test things quickly, but it also can help you save costs. At the end of the workday, you can remove all the resources and reprovision them the next day. To destroy resources in Terraform, simply execute the following command:

```
$ terraform destroy
```

Now, after you have run `terraform destroy` and run `terraform apply` *twice*, you'll notice that the second time you run `terraform apply`, Terraform reports `no changes`, and no action is performed. The next chapter discusses how Terraform decides what actions to take.

There are many more Terraform commands, and we introduce them throughout the book. For now, remember the following four commands:

- `terraform init` to initialize
- `terraform plan` to view and create a Terraform plan
- `terraform apply` to actually provision the resources
- `terraform destroy` to remove all resources

Now that we have described the basic workflow of Terraform and shown how you run Terraform in Google Cloud Shell, let's look at the different ways of running Terraform on your local computer.

Running Terraform in your local environment

While running Terraform in the Cloud Shell is the easiest way to run Terraform, most developers prefer to edit and develop code on their own machine in their local environment.

Terraform provides an easy way to do this. First, install Terraform on your computer. Terraform is available on most platforms, including Linux, macOS, and Windows. To install Terraform, please go to `https://developer.hashicorp.com/terraform/downloads` and follow the installation instructions for your environment.

In this book, we use Terraform on Ubuntu, but the code and the principles are the same regardless of the operating system.

You also require the Google Cloud CLI: `gcloud`. So, if you have not already installed it, please go ahead and do so. To see whether you have successfully installed both, run these commands in your preferred shell on your local machine:

```
$ gcloud --version
$ terraform -version
```

Once you have successfully installed both `gcloud` and Terraform, you need to authenticate Terraform against the Google Cloud project you are using.

Authentication using a service account

> **Note**
> The code for this section is in `chap01/key-file`.

There are several ways to authenticate Terraform with Google Cloud. The first is using a service account. For this, you create a service account and download a key file.

You can create a service account and download the key file interactively using the web console or the following gcloud commands. If you haven't authenticated against Google Cloud in your shell, please do so now using the gcloud auth login command.

Please note that for simplicity's sake, we have given the Terraform service account the broad role of editor. This is not recommended as it violates the security principle of least privilege. You need to replace <PROJECT_ID> with the ID of your Google Cloud project:

```
$ gcloud auth login --no-launch-browser
$ gcloud config set project "<PROJECT_ID>"
$ gcloud iam service-accounts create terraform \
    --description="Terraform Service Account" \
    --display-name="terraform"

$ export GOOGLE_SERVICE_ACCOUNT=`gcloud iam service-accounts \
  list --format="value(email)"  --filter=name:"terraform@"`
$ export GOOGLE_CLOUD_PROJECT=`gcloud info \
--format="value(config.project)"`

$ gcloud projects add-iam-policy-binding $GOOGLE_CLOUD_PROJECT \
    --member="serviceAccount:$GOOGLE_SERVICE_ACCOUNT" \
    --role="roles/editor"

$ gcloud iam service-accounts keys create "./terraform.json"  \
    --iam-account=$GOOGLE_SERVICE_ACCOUNT
```

Once you have a key file, you can reference it in your Terraform configuration using the provider declaration.

As we mentioned, Terraform does not care about filenames. It combines all files with the .tf extension and then creates an execution plan using all the configurations. However, while Terraform doesn't care about filenames, humans do. As one of the objectives of IaC is to share and reuse code, there are commonly adopted file naming conventions. We use those conventions throughout the book.

The convention is to place the provider declaration in a file called provider.tf. We mentioned earlier that Terraform supports several cloud providers and other infrastructure tools. It does so by using the concept of a *provider*. A provider is a translation layer between Terraform and the external API of the provider. When you run Terraform, it translates your configuration code into API calls that interact with the provider—in this case, Google Cloud. If you run Terraform with the AWS provider, it generates AWS API calls.

This is also the reason that while Terraform works with all cloud providers, each configuration file is specific to a particular cloud provider. You cannot use the same code to provision a Google Cloud and an AWS VM. However, the principles of developing and managing Terraform code and the workflow are similar for all cloud providers. Thus, if you have mastered Terraform for Google Cloud, you can use that knowledge to learn Terraform for AWS and Azure.

The Google provider has several optional attributes. The most commonly used attributes are project, region, and zone, which specify the default `project`, `region`, and `zone`. So, the provider file for our example using the credentials file in the current directory looks like this:

> **Note**
> You need to replace <PROJECT_ID> with the project ID of your Google Cloud project.

provider.tf

```
provider "google" {
  project     = <PROJECT_ID>
  region      = "us-central1"
  zone        = "us-central1-c"
  credentials = "./terraform.json"
}
```

Thus, you can now run the Terraform workflow on your local computer, like so:

```
$ terraform init
$ terraform apply
```

Service account keys are very powerful in Google Cloud and must be treated carefully. Thus, we do not recommend including a reference to the credentials and—particularly—storing the key file in the local directory. It is easy to accidentally include the key file in your source code, where it can leak. It also makes the code less portable.

Authentication using a service account and environment variable

> **Note**
> The code for this section is in `chap01/environment-variable`.

A better way is to store the key content in an environment variable, which can, in turn, be stored more securely (for example, via envchain) than plaintext key files on disk, as can be seen in the following command:

```
$ export GOOGLE_CREDENTIALS=`cat ../key-file/terraform.json`
```

Using an environment variable has the added benefit of making your Terraform code more portable, as it does not include the authentication method in the Terraform code.

Service account impersonation

> **Note**
> The code for this section is in chap01/service-account-impersonation.

A third method is to use *service account impersonation*. This Google Cloud concept lets users act as or *impersonate* a service account. To use service account impersonation, you first need to allow you, the user, the **Identity and Access Management (IAM)** role of **Service Account Token Creator** (roles/iam.serviceAccountTokenCreator). Please note that this role is not enabled by default, even for a project owner, so you have to add that IAM role explicitly.

Second, set the GOOGLE_IMPERSONATE_SERVICE_ACCOUNT environment variable to the Terraform service account we created in the previous section. Ensure that the GOOGLE_APPLICATION_CREDENTIALS environment variable is *NOT* set.

Next, acquire the user credentials to use for **Application Default Credentials (ADC)** using the following command:

```
$ gcloud auth application-default login
```

These are credentials that Terraform uses to impersonate the service account and perform other actions on behalf of that service account using the IAM permission of that service account. Please note that this is a separate authentication from the Google platform credentials (gcloud auth login).

As we mentioned, service account keys must be handled with care, thus it is better to delete them if they are not in use. Thus, here is the complete code to impersonate the service account and clean up the environment:

```
# Delete unused credentials locally
$ unset GOOGLE_CREDENTIALS

# Delete previously issued keys
$ rm ../key-file/terraform.json
```

```
$ gcloud iam service-accounts keys list \
--iam-account=$GOOGLE_ SERVICE_ACCOUNT
$ gcloud iam service-accounts keys delete \
<SERVICE_ACCOUNT_ID> --iam-account=$GOOGLE_SERVICE_ACCOUNT

# Set up impersonation
$ export GOOGLE_IMPERSONATE_SERVICE_ACCOUNT=\
`gcloud iam service-accounts list --format="value(email)" \
--filter=name:terraform`

$ gcloud auth application-default login --no-launch-browser

$ export USER_ACCOUNT_ID=`gcloud config get core/account`

$ gcloud iam service-accounts add-iam-policy-binding \
    $GOOGLE_IMPERSONATE_SERVICE_ACCOUNT \
    --member="user:$USER_ACCOUNT_ID" \
    --role="roles/iam.serviceAccountTokenCreator"

$ export GOOGLE_CLOUD_PROJECT=`gcloud info \
--format="value(config.project)"`
```

While this may look tedious, you only need to do it once. Using impersonation makes the code more portable and more secure, as it does not rely on service account keys and does not specify the authentication method in your configuration files. Please note that it might take a couple of minutes for the added IAM role to become effective. But once it is effective, run the following command:

```
$ terraform apply
```

Now that we have shown different ways to authenticate Terraform to Google Cloud and created a simple server, let's provision something more useful. But before we move to the next section, don't forget to destroy the server by running the following command:

```
$ terraform destroy
```

Parameterizing Terraform

> **Note**
>
> The code for this section is in `chap01/parameterizing-terraform`.

So far, we have provisioned a server that doesn't really do anything. To conclude this first chapter, let's expand on it to demonstrate the power of IaC. First, we add variables to make our code more generic. In Terraform, you need to declare variables in a variable block. While you can declare variables anywhere in your code, by convention, it is best to declare them in a file called `variables.tf`. No argument is required for a variable declaration, but it is a good idea to define the type and a description and, if useful, to add a default value. You can also add validation and specify that the variable contains a sensitive value, but more on that later:

variables.tf

```
variable "project_id" {
  type        = string
  description = "ID of the Google Project"
}
variable "region" {
  type        = string
  description = "Default Region"
  default     = "us-central1"
}
variable "zone" {
  type        = string
  description = "Default Zone"
  default     = "us-central1-a"
}
variable "server_name" {
  type        = string
  description = "Name of server"
}
variable "machine_type" {
  type        = string
  description = "Machine Type"
  default   = "e2-micro"
}
```

Variables are referenced using the `var.<variable_name>` syntax. Thus, our parameterized `main.tf` file now looks like this:

main.tf

```
resource "google_compute_instcance" "this" {
  name          = var.server_name
  machine_type  = var.machine_type
  zone          = var.zone

  boot_disk {
    initialize_params {
      image = "debian-cloud/debian-11"
    }
  }
  network_interface {
    network = "default"
    access_config {
      // Ephemeral public IP
    }
  }
  metadata_startup_script = file("startup.sh")
  tags = ["http-server"]
}
```

We made two minor additions to the `google_compute_instance` resource. We added the `access_config` block to the `network_interface` block, which assigns a public IP address to the server, and added an `http-server` network tag. This allows HTTP traffic to reach the server using the `default-allow-http` firewall rule. (Please note that this firewall rule is created the first time you provision a compute instance and enable `Allow HTTP traffic` in the web console or in `gcloud`. Thus, if you haven't done so in your current project, please do so, as Google Cloud automatically creates this firewall rule. Later, we show how to create firewall rules using Terraform).

There are multiple ways to assign a value to a variable. First, you can specify a default value in the declaration. Second, you can pass it as a value either interactively or via the command-line flag. One of the common ways to specify variable values is in the variable definitions file or `.tfvars` file. This file contains only variable assignments for the form `variable = value` form. You will learn the usefulness of `tfvars` in the third chapter:

terraform.tfvars

```
project_id = <PROJECT_ID>
server_name = "parameterizing-terraform"
```

> **Note**
>
> You need to replace <PROJECT_ID> with the ID of your Google Cloud project.

The second change we can make is to configure a web server automatically. As we said earlier, there is some overlap between IaC and configuration management. You can include startup scripts to perform some configuration code once the server is deployed. Configuration management tools provide much more functionality, and you should use the startup scripts only for basic configuration. Alternatively, you can use the startup script to run the configuration management tool. Our startup script installs the Apache web server and adds the obligatory "Hello World" text:

startup.sh

```
#! /bin/bash
apt update
apt -y install apache2
cat <<EOF > /var/www/html/index.html
<html><body><p>Hello World!</p></body></html>
```

Lastly, we can use the output block to output the public IP address of the server (don't worry about the syntax—we elaborate on that later). Again, we use the convention to place the output block in a file named outputs.tf:

outputs.tf

```
output "instance_ip_addr" {
   value = google_compute_instance.this.network_
interface.0.access_config.0.nat_ip
}
```

Thus, you should now have the following files in your current directory:

```
├── main.tf
├── outputs.tf
├── provider.tf
├── startup.sh
├── terraform.tfvars
└── variables.tf
```

Terraform provisions the server, and then output its IP address. Copy the IP address and paste it into a browser. If you get a timeout error, ensure that the `default-allow-http` firewall rule is set.

While we defined the default machine type as `e2-micro`, we can override any variable value on the command line using the `-var` flag.

Thus, the following command provisions the equivalent server but with an `e2-small` machine type:

```
$ terraform destroy
$ terraform apply -var machine_type=e2-small
```

As we conclude this chapter, it is a good idea to clean up your environment and remove servers and resources you don't need anymore. So, if you have not done so, run the following command:

```
$ terraform destroy
```

Confirming that you removed all unnecessary servers using the web console is also a good practice.

Comparing authentication methods

This chapter presented four different methods of running and authenticating Terraform in Google Cloud. The first one is to run Terraform in Google Cloud Shell, which requires no installation or authentication. To run Terraform locally, you need to use a service account using either a key file or service account impersonation.

Managing key files poses a security risk. Key files are not automatically rotated and hence tend to be long-lived. Even if your organization manually rotates key files, they then need to be distributed, which introduces considerable overhead.

Using service account impersonation eliminates the risk associated with generating and distributing service account keys. Service account impersonation also makes code more portable as it does not depend on any external file.

Summary

In this chapter, we introduced the concept of IaC and why it is critical to DevOps. IaC makes the provisioning of cloud resources faster, more consistent, and, ultimately, more secure. There are several IaC tools, but Terraform has emerged as the de facto IaC tool for it is easy to use and, through the concept of providers, can be used with any cloud provider.

You provisioned your first resource in Google Cloud using Terraform in Google Cloud Shell. But as most cloud engineers and architects prefer to use their own machines, you learned three authentication methods for using Terraform on your local PC while provisioning resources in your Google Cloud project. We showed why service account impersonation is the preferred method of authenticating Terraform by eliminating the risks associated with service account keys.

The chapter also introduced variables to make Terraform configurations more flexible and showed the different methods of assigning values to variables.

In the next chapter, you deepen your understanding of Terraform by delving into the inner workings, discussing the concept of the Terraform state, and introducing additional concepts of the Terraform language.

Before you go to the next chapter, make sure that you have removed all servers not to incur any unnecessary costs. The beauty of IaC and Terraform is that you only need to rerun Terraform to recreate resources if you need them again.

2

Exploring Terraform

In this chapter, we continue our exploration of Terraform. We start by explaining the Terraform state and how Terraform uses it to plan which actions it needs to take. We show various commands on how to investigate the current state, and what to watch out for. We then show how teams can collaborate by using the backend state.

We will look at meta-arguments, which are particular Terraform constructs, to enable you to write efficient Terraform code.

In this chapter, we are going to cover the following main topics:

- Understanding the Terraform state
- Using the backend state
- Understanding Terraform meta-arguments
- Using the `self_link` attribute

Technical requirements

We assume you now have a local environment with Terraform and `gcloud` installed and an appropriate Google Cloud project.

The source code for this chapter is located in `chap02` of our GitHub repository: `https://github.com/PacktPublishing/Terraform-for-Google-Cloud-Essential-Guide`. Just as we did in the previous chapter, we placed the code of each section in the corresponding subdirectory.

Understanding the Terraform state

> **Note**
> The code for this section is under `chap02/statefile` in the GitHub repo of this book.

Understanding the concept of **state** is essential to master Terraform. A Terraform configuration is a declaration of the *desired state*—that is, you specify how you want things to be. Terraform's job is to bring the current *state* to the *desired state*.

So, when you started, you specified in your configuration—that is, the collection of `.tf` files—that you would like to have one compute instance. Then, when you run `terraform apply`, Terraform takes the necessary actions to bring the resource address into the desired state. Since you didn't have any compute instance as specified in your configuration file, Terraform created one.

To start this section, run Terraform by executing the following two commands. This provisions the infrastructure where we left off in the last chapter:

```
$ terraform init
$ terraform apply
```

Now, run `terraform apply` again. Terraform determines the difference between the actual state and the desired state. Since the actual state maps to the desired state, Terraform does not need to take any action.

Terraform stores the existing state in the Terraform **state file**. By default, it is stored in a file called `terraform.tfstate` in the current directory. Go ahead and look at it. As it is in *JSON* format, it is human-readable. For this single resource, it is over 100 lines; for even slightly complex deployments, the state file runs into 1,000 lines. Generally speaking, you should never need to read or manipulate the state file directly.

Looking at the state file, you notice it starts with some metadata. It then lists the outputs and the resources. For this single resource of compute instance, it lists all the attributes.

Since the JSON file is just an internal representation of that state and is not meant to be edited or read by humans, Terraform provides several commands to make the state file more accessible and safer to manipulate. `terraform show` prints out the current state file (or plan file) in a human-readable format, but it is usually very lengthy, particularly if you have provisioned multiple resources. The complete state file representation for this single resource is over 70 lines.

The `terraform state list` command is more practical. It lists all the resources in the state file. In our case, it shows a single resource with the **resource address** `google_compute_instance.this`. You notice that the resource address is a concatenation of the resource type (`google_compute_instance`) and the name (`this`).

The `terraform state show ADDRESS` command shows all the attributes of that resource. Thus, in our current state, we can see one resource with the resource address `google_compute_instance.this`:

```
$ terraform state list
google_compute_instance.this
$ terraform state show google_compute_instance.this
# google_compute_instance.this:
resource "google_compute_instance" "this" {
    can_ip_forward          = false
    cpu_platform            = "Intel Broadwell"
    current_status          = "RUNNING"
    deletion_protection     = false
    enable_display          = false
    guest_accelerator       = []
    id                      = "projects/…/zones/us-central1-a/
instances/state-file"
    instance_id             = "497903608900010349"
    label_fingerprint       = "42WmSpB8rSM="
    machine_type            = "e2-micro"
    metadata_fingerprint    = "nb0qL5x7PbM="
…·
```

Terraform uses the **resource address** to uniquely identify resources. For example, `google_compute_instance.this` uniquely identifies the single server that we specified in our configuration. For resource specification, the syntax is `resource_type.resource_name[instance index]`.

Where `resource_type` is the type of resource—that is, `google_compute_instance` and `resource_name` is the name that we gave it—in this case, `this`. If we have a list of resources, `instance_index` identifies the instance within that list. We will show this later in the chapter.

Interacting with the Terraform state

One useful command is `terraform console`, which enables you to interact with the current state. You can execute functions (more on that later), but you can also show parts of the resource. This can be very useful to determine the exact syntax for a particular attribute.

For example, let's say you want to output the public IP address of a server that you provisioned. `google_compute_instance.this` lists all the attributes of that resource. You can see that the IP list is listed in the `network_interface` block but you don't know the exact syntax that is required to list only the IP address.

Using the console, you can examine the attributes of a resource one by one, and traverse the structure of that resource interactively. You can see that `google_compute_instance.this.network_interface` is actually a list (more on that later) as an instance can have more than one network interface. `google_compute_instance.this.network_interface[0].access_config[0]` lists all the attributes of that block and `google_compute_instance.this.network_interface[0].access_config[0].nat_ip` shows the external IP address.

Understanding destructive changes

Once you start working with Terraform and running it repeatedly, it is critical to understand the implications of running Terraform.

Using the web console, you should see a server with the name `state-file`. Add a label to the compute instance, as shown in *Figure 2.1*. Make sure that you click on both **SAVE** buttons, to actually apply the label:

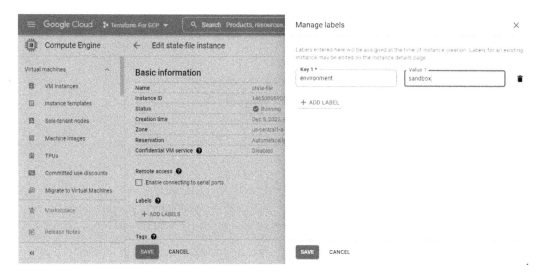

Figure 2.1 – Adding a label using the web console

Now, run `terraform plan`. In the plan, Terraform will inform you that it will **change** one resource. Looking at the detailed plan, Terraform shows that it will change the `labels` attribute by changing the label that you just added to `null`:

```
$ terraform plan
google_compute_instance.this: Refreshing state... [id=projects/
tf-gcp-01/zones/us-central1-a/instances/state-file]
```

```
...
        id                          = "projects/.../zones/
us-central1-a/instances/state-file"
      ~ labels                      = {
          - "environment" = "sandbox" -> null
        }
        name                        = "server-2-1"
        tags                        = [
            "http-server",
        ]
        # (17 unchanged attributes hidden)
        # (4 unchanged blocks hidden)
    }


Plan: 0 to add, 1 to change, 0 to destroy.
...
```

Now, run `terraform apply`, and inspect the compute instance using the web console. You will see that the label is gone. Terraform changed the actual state of your compute engine, which had a label to the desired state, which does not have a label. But nothing else changed.

Now, let's make another change using the web console. This time, remove the startup script. Make sure to hit **SAVE**, and take note of the external IP address. When you run `terraform plan`, the plan will report that it will destroy one resource and add another. If you look at the details, you'll find that the plan says that `google_compute_instance.this` must be replaced. This is known as a *destructive* change.

Run `terraform apply` to perform the change. You will see that Terraform first *destroyed*—meaning it removed the instance—and then *created* a new instance. Note that the public IP address of the instance has changed. Thus, destructive changes can have major consequences.

It takes some time to learn which changes can be performed *in-place*—that is, are *non-destructive*—and which changes are destructive. Thus, you should always look at the Terraform plan and inspect carefully the actions Terraform plans to take to bring the actual state to the desired state.

Avoiding configuration drift

This brings us to an important issue of **Infrastructure as Code (IaC)**, which is known as **configuration drift** (or is sometimes referred to as **environment drift**). Configuration drift occurs when resources are changed, created, or deleted outside of the IaC tool (that is, outside of Terraform).

It is tempting to make changes using the Google Cloud console or the **command-line interface** (**CLI**) because, let's face it, often it is faster. However, this creates problems. At best, the next time you run Terraform, the change will be undone. At worst, a serious configuration drift can take much work to resolve.

Using the Google Cloud console create a new compute instance with the name `instance-1`. Next, run Terraform, but let's give the server the name `instance-1` on the command line using the `-var` argument. It should look like this:

```
$ terraform plan -var "server_name=instance-1" -out plan
```

The summary informs you that Terraform will destroy one resource and add a new one. Looking at the details shown as follows, you see the reason why the instance needs to be replaced is that the name of the server changes from `state-file` to `instance-1`:

```
$ terraform plan -var "server_name=instance-1" -out plan
google_compute_instance.this: Refreshing state...
...


  # google_compute_instance.this must be replaced
-/+ resource "google_compute_instance" "this" {
...

      ~ name                           = "state-file" -> "instance-1"
# forces replacement
```

Now, let's see what happens when we apply the plan (make sure to specify the generated plan). Here's the command to do so:

```
$ terraform apply plan
```

First, Terraform deletes the compute instance named `state-file` as expected. However, Terraform then throws up an error that an instance with the name `instance-1` already exists.

This illustrates two issues. First, Terraform can only look at the resources that it knows exist—that is, the resources in the state file. Terraform has no knowledge that a server with the name `instance-1` exists, so it goes ahead and takes action to create it.

Now, Terraform actually makes calls to the Google API. Thus, when Terraform attempts to create a server with the name `instance-1`, the Google API reports an error as you cannot have two compute engines with the same name and reports that back to Terraform.

So, at plan time, Terraform only *knows* about resources created through Terraform. Later in the book, you will learn how to *import* existing resources into the state, but we should caution you that this is fraught with its own set of issues.

The second issue is that Terraform destroyed the existing server before attempting to create a new one (which failed), so we are left with no servers (as far as Terraform is concerned).

Now, let's recreate the destroyed server. Since we are using IaC, this is as easy as running the following command:

```
$ terraform apply
```

This will create a new compute instance with the default name of state-file, shown as follows:

```
$ terraform state list
```

It then gives us a list of resources in the state. Now, we can remove the resource from the state file using the following command:

```
$ terraform state rm google_compute_instance.this
```

It is essential to understand that while the resource was removed from the state file, it was not actually removed from Google Cloud. Go to the web console to see that the state-file server still exists. Now, if we run terraform plan and terraform apply, the same error as before would be incurred. Terraform will plan to create a new **virtual machine** (**VM**) (Compute Engine), but when it actually tries to create it, it will report an error as the server already exists. It is just that Terraform didn't know about the existence of the server.

Thus, there are two important lessons. First, you should not add or remove resources to the state file unless in exceptional circumstances. Second, once you use Terraform (or any other IaC tool), you should not use the Google Cloud console or the CLI to make changes. All changes must be done through the configuration file in Terraform.

Additional state commands

Now, sometimes you want to force Terraform to replace a resource. The terraform taint ADDRESS command will **taint** a resource—that is, it labels it so that the next time Terraform is run, the resource will be removed and rebuilt. Thus, go to the web console and remove all compute instances. Then, run terraform apply to recreate the server and put it in the Terraform state:

```
$ terraform apply
$ terraform plan
```

When you now run terraform plan, Terraform does not detect any changes. Now, execute the following command:

```
$ terraform taint google_compute_instance.this
$ terraform plan
```

If you now run `terraform plan`, Terraform reports that it will replace the instance. `terraform untaint` removes the taint.

Occasionally, Terraform informs you of the changes in the metadata of Google resources that might cause changes to occur when you generate a plan or call `apply` next. Thus, it is a good idea to occasionally run `terraform refresh`, which updates the current state with the latest metadata.

Using the backend state

> **Note**
>
> The code for this section is under `chap02/backend` in the GitHub repo of this book.

By default, the **Terraform state** is stored locally in the current directory in a file called `terraform.tfstate`. This is fine as long as you are the only one working on the Terraform code and you are always working on the same machine. However, most of the time, you are part of a team that works jointly on the cloud infrastructure. If everybody stored their own version of the state file, chaos would ensue.

To enable collaboration, Terraform allows remote storage of the state file using the concept of **state backends**. (Please note that this is different from remote states, which we discuss in *Chapter 5, Managing Environments with Terraform.*) For Google Cloud, the remote backend is stored in **Google Cloud Storage**. Thus, instead of the state file being stored locally, the state file is stored in a Cloud Storage bucket where all team members (with the right permission) can access the state file. Furthermore, backends support **locking** so that only one member can run Terraform at a time. When `terraform apply` is run, Terraform places a lock in Cloud Storage and only releases the lock once it has completed all actions. If another person or process attempts to run Terraform while the lock is in place, Terraform reports an error and does not execute.

To specify a backend, create a file named `backend.tf` (as we mentioned, naming in Terraform is largely irrelevant, but the backend is specified in a file called `backend.tf` by convention):

chap02/backend/backend.tf

```
terraform {
  backend "gcs" {
    bucket = "<PROJECT_ID>-tf-state"
    prefix  = " chap02/backend"
  }
}
```

Now, the bucket must exist beforehand. Thus, this is one of the few times you should create a resource outside of Terraform using the Google Cloud console or `gcloud`. The bucket should not be part of the current state file, and you only have to create the bucket once per project. Now, since buckets have to be uniquely named, an easy way to ensure there is no naming conflict is to use the project name followed by the suffix `tf-state`. We use this convention throughout the remainder of this book. Thus, whenever you create a new project, please remember to create the corresponding bucket to store the state file remotely.

You can use a `prefix` attribute to place the state file in a folder of the bucket. It is also a good idea to enable **versioning** so that you can recover the state in case anything goes wrong.

If you have previously applied any infrastructure changes locally, they are stored in the local state file. Thus, the first time after you specify the backend, Terraform asks you whether you want to migrate the existing state from the local directory to the backend. Now, run `terraform apply`. While Terraform is running, go to the cloud storage using the web console and observe the contents of your bucket. You see a file named `default.tflock` appearing and disappearing once Terraform has completed its run. (Please note that the `.tflock` file only exists while Terraform is running, so it might disappear rather quickly.):

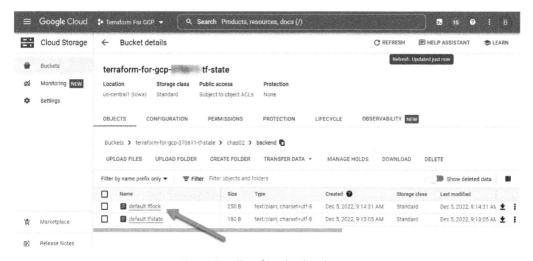

Figure 2.2 – Terraform backend state

Now that you have a good understanding of the Terraform state and when you should use a backend state, let's move to additional concepts in Terraform.

Understanding Terraform meta-arguments

Meta-arguments are special constructs in Terraform. You already encountered the `provider` meta-argument, but let's look closely at it and other meta-arguments.

The provider meta-argument

> **Note**
> The code for this section is under `chap02/provider` in the GitHub repo of this book.

We introduced the `provider` meta-argument in the first chapter. Technically speaking, a provider is a plugin that communicates with the external API—in our case, the Google Cloud API. As mentioned, there are actually two providers for Google Cloud: `google` and `google-beta`. The latter provides the interface to the Google Beta API while the former provides the interface to the API that is in **General Availability** (**GA**). You can use both providers in your configuration code, and specify which provider you want to use for a resource:

chap02/provider/provider.tf

```
...
provider "google" {
  project = var.project_id
  region  = var.region
  zone    = var.zone
}
provider "google-beta" {
  project = var.project_id
  region  = var.region
  zone    = var.zone
}
```

chap02/provider/main.tf

```
resource "google_compute_instance" "ga-server" {
  provider = google
....

resource "google_compute_instance" "beta-server" {
  provider = google-beta
...
```

In addition, you can have other providers in your configuration. For example, Terraform has a provider for Kubernetes, which provides an alternative to `kubectl`, the default tool to interact with Kubernetes. Thus, you can use the Kubernetes provider in your configuration code by specifying the `kubernetes` provider, and then use Terraform to provision resources both in Google Cloud and in your Kubernetes cluster.

It is recommended that you only combine providers that are related to each other. Generally, try not to mix and match providers in the same configuration unless you have a good reason for it.

As we mentioned, Terraform and its providers have a very dynamic developer community—that is, new versions are constantly released. Thus, it is good practice to place version constraints on both Terraform and the provider. The place to do so is in the Terraform block (`https://www.terraform.io/language/settings`), which is usually inserted in the `provider.tf` file. The `required_version` settings set a version constraint on the Terraform version, whereas the `required_providers` block specifies the source of the provider and the version constraint, as shown in the following code snippet:

chap02/provider/provider.tf

```
terraform {
  required_version = "~> 1.3.0"
  required_providers {
    google = {
      source  = "hashicorp/google"
      version = "~> 4.40"
    }
  }
}
provider "google" {
  project = var.project_id
  region  = var.region
  zone    = var.zone
}
```

While not absolutely required, it is good practice to include the Terraform block and the version constraint, and we will do so from now on.

The count meta-argument

> **Note**
>
> The code for this section is under `chap02/count` in the GitHub repo of this book.

Often, you will find yourself wanting to create (nearly) identical resources—for example, several web servers. You could copy the code multiple times, but that would be tedious and make maintenance of the code more difficult. The `count` meta-argument provides the capability to create identical resources in a single block. Let's examine the following code:

chap2/count/main.tf

```
resource "google_compute_instance" "this" {
  provider      = google
  count         = 3
  name          = "${var.server_name}-${count.index}"
  machine_type  = var.machine_type
  zone          = var.zone

  boot_disk {
    initialize_params {
      image = "debian-cloud/debian-11"
    }
  }
  network_interface {
    network = "default"
    access_config {
      // Ephemeral public IP
    }
  }
  metadata_startup_script = file("startup.sh")

  tags = ["http-server"]
}
```

We use the `count` meta-argument to specify that we want to have three servers. Let's take a look at the fourth line, the one we highlighted:

```
name          = "${var.server_name}-${count.index}"
```

As you know, Google Cloud requires a unique name for each compute engine. We can generate a unique name using the `count.index` construct, which provides an index starting at 0. Here, we also are introducing a new syntax called `interpolation`. Interpolation *"...evaluates the expression given between the markers, converts the result to a string if necessary, and then inserts it into the final string"* (`https://www.terraform.io/language/expressions/strings`).

Thus, as we set the `server_name` variable to `webserver` in `terraforms.tfvars`, `"${var.server_name}-${count.index}"` produces the following strings:

- `webserver-0`
- `webserver-1`
- `webserver-2`

Interpolation is useful when you want to concatenate strings to produce unique names.

The for_each meta-argument

> **Note**
> The code for this section is under `chap02/for-each` in the GitHub repo of this book.

While the `count` meta-argument is helpful in creating nearly identical resources, there are times when you want to create multiple instances of resources that have more variations. That is where the `for_each` meta-argument comes in handy. The `for_each` meta-argument takes a map or set of strings as input and creates a distinct resource for each item.

Let's illustrate the use of `for_each` with a real-life example. Google recommends deleting the default network as a best practice (`https://cloud.google.com/architecture/framework/security/network-security#disable_default_networks`) and defining a custom network. To create a new network, you define several subnets in different regions with different **Classless Inter-Domain Routing** (**CIDR**) ranges.

Let's assume you want to create a new **virtual private cloud** (**VPC**) with different subnets. You could create three `google_compute_subnetwork` resources. Now, if you want to add a fourth subnet, you have to add yet another resource. Instead, we can define a map variable with the subnets and the required information. We can then use the `for_each` meta-argument to reiterate over that map:

chap02/for-each/terraform.tfvars

```
network = "my-network"
subnets = {
  south-carolina = {"region" : "us-east1", "ip_cidr_range" :
"192.168.2.0/24" },
```

```
    iowa = {"region" : "us-central1", "ip_cidr_range" :
"192.168.1.0/24" },
    singapore = {"region" : "asia-southeast1", "ip_cidr_range" :
"192.168.3.0/24" },
}
```

After this, we can use a single resource definition to define all of our subnets, regardless of the number of subnets:

chap02/for-each/vpc.tf

```
resource "google_compute_network" "this" {
  project                 = var.project_id
  name                    = var.network
  auto_create_subnetworks = false
}


resource "google_compute_subnetwork" "this" {
  project                  = var.project_id
  for_each                 = var.subnets
  network                  = var.network
  name                     = each.key
  region                   = each.value["region"]
  ip_cidr_range            = each.value["ip_cidr_range"]
  private_ip_google_access = "true"
}
```

We use the for_each meta-argument and the each.key and each.value addresses to reference the values in the map. Terraform then creates a unique resource for each entry in the map. So, run terraform apply to create a custom VPC. If you get an error, just run terraform apply again. We address the error in the next meta-argument.

Now, you can achieve the same using count and lists. For example, using the count meta-argument, you can define the appropriate firewall rules, like this:

chap02/for-each/firewall.tf

```
resource "google_compute_firewall" "firewall" {
  count   = length(var.firewall)
  network = google_compute_network.this.id
```

```
  name     = "${google_compute_network.this.name}-${var.
firewall[count.index]["name"]}"

  direction = var.firewall[count.index]["direction"]
  allow {
    protocol = var.firewall[count.index]["allow"]["protocol"]
    ports    = var.firewall[count.index]["allow"]["ports"]
  }
  source_ranges = var.firewall[count.index]["source_ranges"]
  target_tags   = var.firewall[count.index]["target_tags"]
}
```

And then, you can specify a list of firewall rules in `terraform.tfvars`:

chap02/for-each/terraform.tfvars

```
firewall = [
  {
    "name" : "allow-all-internal",
    "direction" : "INGRESS",
    "allow" : {
      "protocol" : "all",
      "ports" : []
    },
    "source_ranges" : ["192.168.0.0/16"],
    "target_tags" : [],
  },
  {
    "name" : "allow-http",
    "direction" : "INGRESS",
    "allow" : {
      "protocol" : "tcp",
      "ports" : ["80"]
    },
    "source_ranges" : ["0.0.0.0/0"],
```

```
    "target_tags" : ["http-server"],
  },
]
```

However, there is a difference. Change the order of the subnet map and the firewall list in `terraform.tfvars`. That is, change the subnet map so that the `singapore` entry comes first and change the firewall list so that the `allow-http` rule comes first. Then, run `terraform apply -auto-approve`.

The subnet resources remain the same, but the firewall rules are replaced. That is because in a list, the order matters, whereas in a map, the order does not matter.

Thus, use the `count` meta-argument when the resources are nearly identical but use `for_each` when they are different. In either case, use them with caution because while it's true that you can create very compact code, it can become hard to understand for somebody else reading your code.

The depends_on meta-argument

You probably encountered an error when you ran Terraform the first time in the last section, but when you reran it a minute or two later, you didn't encounter this error. Let's investigate what happened and how we can mitigate it.

When you ran `terraform apply` the first time, you probably received an error message, shown as follows:

```
| Error: Error creating Subnetwork: googleapi: Error 404: The
resource 'projects/.../global/networks/my-network' was not found,
notFound
```

Terraform is quite good at determining the order in which it needs to create resources. Thus, it knows that it must create a network before creating a subnetwork and both before creating a compute instance.

If you look at the output of the `apply` step, you can observe the progress of the creation of the resources. Terraform logs when it starts and completes the creation of a resource:

```
google_compute_network.this: Creating...
google_compute_network.this: Still creating... [10s elapsed]
...
google_compute_network.this: Creation complete after 11s
...
google_compute_subnetwork.this["singapore"]: Creating...
google_compute_subnetwork.this["singapore"]: Still creating...
[10s elapsed]
```

```
google_compute_subnetwork.this["singapore"]: Still creating...
[20s elapsed]
google_compute_subnetwork.this["singapore"]: Creation complete
after 24s
```

However, you might also notice that Terraform creates resources in parallel. That is, it does not wait for a resource's creation to be completed before it starts a new creation. By default, Terraform runs 10 resource operations in parallel.

In our case, Terraform tried to create a subnetwork before the network was fully provisioned, and hence it threw up an error. The second time you ran `terraform apply`, the network was fully provisioned; hence, a subnetwork was created with no error.

Now, we could force Terraform to provision resources one at a time by limiting the number of parallel operations to one. You can do that by using the `-parallelism=n` argument, shown as follows:

```
$ terraform apply -parallelism=1
```

However, that is not very efficient as it takes much longer to provision all the resources. Instead, you can explicitly declare a dependency to ensure that Terraform waits for the resource to be created before attempting to create the other resource. In our case, we can explicitly declare that a network has to be created before Terraform creates a subnetwork.

So, we can add a line with the `depends_on` meta-argument that takes a list of resources as an argument. That is, the resources in that list need to be completely provisioned before the creation of that resource starts:

chap02/for_each/vpc.tcf

```
resource "google_compute_subnetwork" "this" {
  depends_on              = [resource.google_compute_network.
this]
    project               = var.project_id
    for_each              = var.subnets
  network                 = var.network
    name                  = each.key
    region                = each.value["region"]
    ip_cidr_range         = each.value["ip_cidr_range"]
    private_ip_google_access = "true"
}
```

Thus, Terraform now explicitly waits for the network to be completed before creating subnetworks.

Generally speaking, the `depends_on` meta-argument is considered an escape hatch when the provider does not allow you to draw more logical dependency. Using the same example, we can avoid that escape hatch if we replace `network = var.network` with `network = resource.google_compute_network.this.name`. This achieves the same result as it makes the dependency explicit.

There is one more meta-argument that we need to discuss: the `lifecycle` meta-argument.

The lifecycle meta-argument

> **Note**
> The code for this section is under `chap02/lifecycle` in the GitHub repo of this book.

When Terraform needs to change a resource, it will do so in-place. This is known as a non-destructive change. However, when an in-place change is not possible, Terraform will first destroy the current resource and then recreate it with the change applied. Using the `lifecycle` meta-argument, you can change this behavior.

If `create_before_destroy` is set to `true`, Terraform attempts to create a new resource before it destroys it. We show how this can be useful in *Chapter 6, Deploying a Traditional Three-Tier Architecture*.

You can also use the `lifecycle` meta-argument to prevent a resource to be deleted. This is useful in preventing accidental data loss. If `prevent_destroy` is set to `true`, Terraform reports an error when attempting to destroy a resource, and it will not destroy the resource.

The third attribute in this block, `ignore_changes`, can also be very useful. Let's say your cloud environment uses a third-party tool that uses labels to store information. Then, whenever you run Terraform, it performs an update-in-place operation and resets the labels. When we include the `ignore_changes` meta-argument, Terraform will ignore changes to any attribute in the list in applying its `lifecycle` rules:

chap02/lifecycle/main.tf

```
resource "google_compute_instance" "this" {
...
  tags = ["http-server"]
  lifecycle {
    ignore_changes = [
      labels,
    ]
```

```
    }
}
```

Run the code in the `chap02/lifecycle` subdirectory. Then add a label to the instance named `lifecycle`. Now, when you run `terraform plan`, Terraform removes the label. However, when you have the lifecycle rule as shown in the preceding code snippet, Terraform ignores any changes to the label and does not change the instance.

Meta-arguments are integral to the Terraform language and are used with all cloud providers. Before we conclude the chapter, let's look at one concept unique to Google Cloud.

Using the self_link attribute

> **Note**
> The code for this section is under `chap02/self-link` in the GitHub repo of this book.

In the `for_each` example, we used the `name` attribute of the `subnetwork` resource to specify the subnet for our VM:

```
subnetwork = google_compute_subnetwork.this['iowa'].name
```

In Google Cloud, nearly every resource has a unique name, but it is better to use the `self_link` attribute, which is a unique Google Cloud construct. To understand `self_link`, let's look at the details of the `Iowa` subnet using the `gcloud` command:

```
$ gcloud compute networks subnets describe iowa \
--region us-central1
. .
gatewayAddress: 192.168.1.1
id: '4434945742234922953'
ipCidrRange: 192.168.1.0/24
. .
selfLink: https://www.googleapis.com/compute/v1/projects/
tf-gcp-01/regions/us-central1/subnetworks/iowa
stackType: IPV4_ONLY
```

Then look at the same resource using the `terraform state show` command:

```
$ terraform state show    'google_compute_subnetwork.
this["iowa"]'
# google_compute_subnetwork.this["iowa"]:
```

```
resource "google_compute_subnetwork" "this" {
...

    gateway_address           = "192.168.1.1"
...

    ip_cidr_range             = "192.168.1.0/24"
    name                      = "iowa"
  ...
  self_link                   = "https://www.googleapis.com/
compute/v1/projects/tf-gcp-01/regions/us-central1/subnetworks/
iowa"
    stack_type                = "IPV4_ONLY"
}
```

You see that the Terraform state lists much of the same information as the gcloud command including the self_link attribute, which is a **unique identifier** (**UID**) containing additional information. Thus, it is good practice to refer to resources using the self_link attribute, and we use that from now onward.

Summary

In this chapter, we discussed how Terraform uses the state to keep track of the current resources and to decide which actions it needs to perform to bring the current state to the desired state. A thorough understanding of the state is critical to mastering Terraform and anticipating what Terraform will do. We also introduced the concept of the backend where you store the Terraform state in Google Cloud Storage so that teams can collaborate without stepping on each other's toes. We recommend that you use backend states even if you work by yourself. Storing the Terraform state in Google Cloud Storage guarantees that it will never get lost, and if you enable versioning in your bucket, you can retrieve older versions if necessary.

We then introduced *meta-arguments*, which are special Terraform constructs to influence the behavior of Terraform and help to write Terraform code more efficiently.

In the next chapter, we continue our exploration of Terraform by introducing expressions and functions that help you write more efficient Terraform code.

3

Writing Efficient Terraform Code

While Terraform is a declarative language, there are times when you need to use functional constructs to write efficient code. In this chapter, we cover some of these constructs and provide some tips to write Terraform code efficiently. In particular, we introduce dynamic blocks and conditional expressions to make the code more flexible. Then, we show how to use Terraform's built-in functions and information from resources created outside of Terraform. We conclude the chapter by discussing how to expose Terraform information using output values and provide some tricks for writing Terraform code efficiently. Thus, by the end of this chapter, you will be able to write more efficient Terraform code and do so more efficiently.

In this chapter, we cover the following main topics:

- Terraform types and values
- Using Terraform expressions
- Terraform functions
- Referencing existing data using data sources
- Using output values
- Tips to develop Terraform code efficiently

Technical requirements

There are no new technical requirements for this chapter. The code for this chapter can be found at https://github.com/PacktPublishing/Terraform-for-Google-Cloud-Essential-Guide/tree/main/chap03. As usual, we recommend that you run terraform destroy before moving to the next subsection to remove any resources you created, to avoid unnecessary costs.

Terraform types and values

> **Note**
>
> The code for this section is under `chap03/types` in the GitHub repo of this book.

Before we go into expressions, let's have a closer look at Terraform types and values. We have used Terraform types in the variable declarations. Terraform has the following types:

- String
- Number
- Bool(ean)
- List
- Map

The first three are self-explanatory. Lists are sequences of values denoted by square brackets (`[` and `]`) and separated by commas. Maps are groups of named values—that is, `name = value`. A map is surrounded by curly brackets (`{` and `}`) and separated by commas. Lists and maps can also be nested. The following are some common types as defined in a variable definition file:

---

chap03/type/terraform.tfvars

```
string = "This is a string"
number = 14
bool    = true
list    = ["us-west1", "us-west2"]
map     = { us-west1 = "Oregon", us-west2 = "Los Angeles" }
nested_map = {
   americas = ["us-west1", "us-west2"]
   apac     = ["asia-south1", "asia-southeast1"]
}
```

Elements in a list are referenced by their index position, starting with 0. For example, `var.list[1]` refers to the second element in the list. Elements in a map are referenced by their name using the dot notation—for example, `var.map.us-west1`.

Objects are like maps but set constraints on the variable. In the following code segment, we define a variable object to contain two strings—name and `location`—and a list of strings called `regions`. If those three elements are not supplied, then Terraform reports an error. This is particularly useful in modules, which we will introduce in the next chapter:

chap03/type/variables.tf

```
variable "object" {
  type = object({
    name     = string
    location = string
    regions  = list(string)
  })
}
```

Terraform has a special `null` value, which represents absence. We use this value later in this chapter.

Using Terraform expressions

In Terraform, you use an **expression** to refer to a value within a configuration. Thus, a **string** such as `"abc"` or a **list** such as `["orange", "apple", "strawberry"]` is considered a simple expression. However, some expressions are more complex and are helpful when writing more flexible Terraform code. Terraform provides two useful constructs to write more flexible code: **dynamic blocks** and **conditional expressions**.

Dynamic blocks

> **Note**
> The code for this section is under `chap03/dynamic-block` in the GitHub repo of this book.

In the previous chapter, we introduced the ability to create multiple instances using the `count` and `for_each` meta-arguments. Both constructs, in essence, created multiple resources using a single block. Blocks within blocks are termed **nested blocks**, and some nested blocks can be repeated. For example, within the `google_compute_instance` resource, you can attach multiple disks using the `attached_disk` block. Let's say we want to create a server and attach multiple disks to that server. We want to use a variable so that we can keep the disk size and disk type, as well as the attached mode, flexible. Using a variable also allows us to easily change the number of disks.

First, you create multiple disks using a map variable:

chap03/dynamic-block/terraform.tfvars

```
project_id  = <PROJECT_ID>
server_name = "dynamic-block"

disks = {
  small-disk = { "type" : "pd-ssd", "size" : 10, "mode" :
"READ_WRITE" },
  medium-disk = { "type" : "pd-balanced", "size" : 50, "mode" :
"READ_WRITE" },
  large-disk = { "type" : "pd-standard", "size" : 100, "mode" :
"READ_ONLY" },
}
```

Then, you use the `for_each` meta-argument to create the disks:

chap03/dynamic-block/disks.tf

```
resource "google_compute_disk" "this" {
  for_each = var.disks
  name    = each.key
  type    = each.value["type"]
  size    = each.value["size"]
  zone    = var.zone
}
```

Now, we could attach a disk to the server by repeating the `attached_disk` block, shown as follows:

chap03/dynamic-block/main.tf

```
resource "google_compute_instance" "this" {
  name         = var.server_name
  machine_type = var.machine_type
  zone         = var.zone

  boot_disk {
    initialize_params {
```

```
      image = "debian-cloud/debian-11"
    }
  }
  attached_disk {
    source = google_compute_disk.this[«small-disk»].name
    mode   = var.disks[«small-disk»][«mode»]
  }

  attached_disk {
    source = google_compute_disk.this["medium-disk"].name
    mode   = var.disks["medium-disk"]["mode"]
  }

  attached_disk {
    source = google_compute_disk.this["large-disk"].name
    mode   = var.disks["large-disk"]["mode"]
  }
  network_interface {
    network = "default"
    access_config {
      // Ephemeral public IP
    }
  }
}
```

However, that creates two problems. First, we would have to repeat the `attached_disk` block. Second, and more critically, we could not keep the number of disks flexible. If we wanted to attach two or four disks to a server, we would need to change our code depending on the number of attached disks.

To address this issue, Terraform provides a concept of a **dynamic block** (`https://www.terraform.io/language/expressions/dynamic-blocks`). A dynamic block enables you to repeat **nested blocks** within a top-level block. It is best to illustrate this by fixing the issues highlighted previously:

chap03/dynamic-block/main.tf

```
resource "google_compute_instance" "this" {
  name         = var.server_name
  machine_type = var.machine_type
```

```
zone           = var.zone

boot_disk {
  initialize_params {
    image = «debian-cloud/debian-11»
  }
}

dynamic "attached_disk" {
  for_each = var.disks
  content {
    source = google_compute_disk.this[attached_disk.key].name
    mode   = attached_disk.value["mode"]
  }
}
network_interface {
  network = «default»
  access_config {
    // Ephemeral public IP
  }
}
}
```

You define a dynamic block with the keyword `dynamic` followed by a label. The label specifies the kind of nested block—in our case, `attached_disk`. You use the `for_each` construct to iterate over the values, and the `content` keyword defines the body of the nested block. Within the body, you use the label of the `attached_disk` dynamic block and the `value` attribute to refer to the value of the item. Thus, `attached_disk.value` refers to the `var.disks` variable, and `attached_disk.value["name"]` refers to `small-disk`, `medium-disk`, and `large-disk`, respectively.

Thus, using a dynamic block enables you to write multiple repeated blocks by defining the block only once.

Conditional expressions

> **Note**
>
> The code for this section is under the `chap03/conditional-expression` directory in the GitHub repository of this book.

Another concept that can be used to write efficient and flexible Terraform code is a conditional expression (https://www.terraform.io/language/expressions/conditionals). The syntax of conditional expressions is straightforward:

```
condition ? true_val : false_val
```

Such an expression is handy when combined with the `count` meta-argument to decide whether to create a resource or not. Let's say you want the flexibility of assigning either a static or an ephemeral (temporary) IP address to our server. We declare a Boolean variable called `static_ip`. When set to `true`, we create a static IP address and assign it. When set to `false`, we do not create a static IP and assign an ephemeral IP address:

chap03/conditional-expression/main.tf

```
resource "google_compute_address" "static" {
  count = var.static_ip ? 1 : 0
  name  = "ipv4-address"
}


resource "google_compute_instance" "this" {
  name          = var.server_name
  machine_type  = var.machine_type
  zone          = var.zone

  boot_disk {
    initialize_params {
      image = "debian-cloud/debian-11"
    }
  }
  network_interface {
    network = "default"
    access_config {
      nat_ip = var.static_ip ? google_compute_address.
static[0].address : null
    }
  }
}
```

You can see that we use a conditional expression twice. First, we use it in conjunction with the `count` meta-argument. When the `static_ip` variable is set to `false`, the expression evaluates to 0, and no static IP address is created. If set to `true`, the expression evaluates to 1, and hence one static IP address is provisioned.

In the `access_config` block, we again use a conditional expression. If the variable is set to `true`, we use the attribute of the `google_compute_address.static` resource to assign the `NAT_IP` address. If set to `false`, then we assign a `null` value, and Terraform assigns an ephemeral IP address.

Test it out by switching the value of the `static_ip` variable, and then, using the web console, look at the external IP of the **virtual machine** (**VM**):

```
$ terraform apply -var static_ip=false
$ terraform apply -var static_ip=true
```

But let's assume we either want to assign a static *external* IP address or *no external* IP address at all. This is where we can use the `null` value to our advantage, as illustrated in the following code example:

```
resource "google_compute_address" "static" {
  count = var.static_ip ? 1 : 0
  name  = "ipv4-address"
}
resource "google_compute_instance" "this" {
  name         = var.server_name
  machine_type = var.machine_type
  zone         = var.zone

  boot_disk {
    initialize_params {
      image = "debian-cloud/debian-11"
    }
  }

  network_interface {
    network = "default"
    dynamic "access_config" {
      for_each = google_compute_address.static
      content {
        nat_ip = google_compute_address.static[0].address
      }
```

```
        }
      }
    }
```

Let's examine the highlighted code. First, we use a dynamic block, as indicated by the dynamic keyword. Then, we use a for_each construct to loop over the value of the google_compute_address. static resource. If no resource was created, this evaluates to the null value, so Terraform does not generate any block. If var.static_ip is set to true, then google_compute_address. static has a value that we loop over and assign the static IP address, as in the previous example.

So now, if you run the following code, you see that the server does not have any external IP address at all:

```
$ terraform apply -var static_ip=false
```

However, if you set the static_ip variable to true, the server has a static external IP address:

```
$ terraform apply -var static_ip=true
```

You often find yourself in positions where you need to create or transform expressions, and for that, Terraform provides **built-in** functions.

Terraform functions

Terraform has a number of built-in functions that you can utilize to create or transform expressions. One of the best ways to learn them is to use Terraform interactively using the terraform console command. We introduced this command earlier to investigate the state interactively. Here is another way to use Terraform interactively and learn about functions:

```
$ terraform console
> max(2,3)
3
> lower("HELLO WORLD")
"hello world"
> index(["apple", "orange", "banana"], "orange")
1
> formatdate("HH:mm",timestamp())
"01:32"
```

The general syntax for Terraform functions is function_name(argument_1, argument_2, ..., argument_n). Terraform has a variety of built-in functions, including string, data, numeric, and filesystem functions. Please refer to the documentation at https://www.terraform.io/language/functions for a complete reference.

Referencing existing data using data sources

> **Note**
> The code for this section is under `chap03/data-source` in the GitHub repo of this book.

We discussed earlier that you should not mix provisioning resources through Terraform and the Google Cloud console, as this can lead to configuration drift. However, there are cases when you want to use information from data that Google Cloud provides or cloud resources that are created outside of your configuration file or out of your control. Terraform provides data sources, which you can read more about here: `https://www.terraform.io/language/data-sources`.

If you look at the Google Terraform documentation, available here at `https://registry.terraform.io/providers/hashicorp/google/latest/docs`, you'll see a list of Google Cloud services that you can provision using Terraform. Under each service, you generally find a **resources** and a **data sources** subsection. Resources let you provision and manage Google Cloud resources, whereas data sources let you retrieve information from existing Google Cloud resources.

For example, the `google_compute_instance` resource (`https://registry.terraform.io/providers/hashicorp/google/latest/docs/resources/compute_instance`) creates a new VM instance, whereas the `google_compute_instance` data source (`https://registry.terraform.io/providers/hashicorp/google/latest/docs/data-sources/compute_instance`) lets you reference an existing VM instance that was created outside of your Terraform configuration.

Go to the web console to create a new compute instance. Use all the default values, including the name of `instance-1`.

Then, you can retrieve all the information of that VM instance using the `google_compute_instance` data source, as seen in the following code snippet. Once instantiated, you can reference any attribute of that instance as if you had created the instance within Terraform. For example, you can output the IP address of that instance as we did before:

chap03/datasource/data.tf

```
data "google_compute_instance" "this" {
  name = "instance-1"
}
output "ip-address" {
  value = format("IP address of existing server: %s", data.
google_compute_instance.this.network_interface[0].access_
config[0].nat_ip)
}
```

Some data sources give you access to information from your current Google project or organization. Let's say you want to create several servers and distribute them evenly across the zones in a region.

Your first inclination is probably to use the region name and a letter as that is the naming convention of Google zones—for example, us-central1-a.

However, while most Google Cloud regions have three zones, there are some regions with four. Furthermore, the zones are not consistently named. For example, the three Singapore zones are named asia-southeast1-a, asia-southeast1-b, and asia-southeast1-c, whereas the zones in us-east1 are named us-east1-b, us-east1-c, and us-east1-d.

For this, you can use the google_compute_zones data source with no arguments. This data source retrieves all the zones in the current region as a list. Thus, once instantiated, you can then reference the zone using the name attribute, as shown in the following code snippet:

chap03/datasource/main.tf

```
data "google_compute_zones" "available" {
}
resource "google_compute_instance" "this" {
  count         = var.instance_number
  name          = var.server_name
  machine_type  = var.machine_type
  zone          = data.google_compute_zones.available.
names[count.index % length(data.google_compute_zones.available.
names)]

  boot_disk {
    initialize_params {
      image = "debian-cloud/debian-11"
    }
  }
  network_interface {
    network = "default"
    access_config {
    }
  }
}
output "zones" {
  value = [for s in google_compute_instance.this[*] : "${s.
```

```
  name}: ${s.zone}"]
  }
```

Give it a try by running `terraform plan` for different regions. Here's an example:

```
$ terraform plan -var region=us-central1
$ terraform plan -var region=asia-southeast1
```

We introduce more data sources in the following chapters. Understanding the difference between data sources and resources is essential since they often share the same name. **Resources** create new resources, whereas **data sources** expose information about existing resources. However, using a data source does not import an existing resource into the Terraform state, nor can you manage resources using data sources. You can only extract information from existing resourcing using data sources.

Using output values

> **Note**
>
> The code for this section is under `chap03/output` in the GitHub repo of this book.

We used output values briefly but have not yet discussed them in detail. Output values expose information from Terraform. So far, we have used them to output IP addresses or other pertinent information on the command line. However, output values do more, as we see in the following chapters.

By convention, all output values are placed in a file called `outputs.tf`. An output block requires a `label` argument and an argument named `value` that outputs the value of an expression. The `description` argument is optional and is used to describe a short description of the output.

Now is also an excellent opportunity to introduce the **splat expression** (`https://www.terraform.io/language/expressions/splat`). A splat expression is a short form of a `for` expression and is best explained by the following example. The two highlighted code segments are equivalent. Splat expressions are useful in combination with other loop constructs—for example, `[for s in google_compute_instance.this[*] : "${s.name}: ${s.zone}"]`:

chap03/output/outputs.tf

```
output "zones-splat" {
  description = "List of zones using a splat expression"
  value       = google_compute_instance.this[*].zone
}

output "zones-for" {
```

```
  description = "List of zones using a for loop
  value       = [for server in google_compute_instance.this :
server.zone]
}
output "zones-by-servers" {
  description = "Name of zone for each server"
  value       = [for s in google_compute_instance.this[*] :
"${s.name}: ${s.zone}"]
}
output "URL_0" {
  description = "URL of first server"
  value       = format("http://%s", google_compute_instance.
this[0].network_interface[0].access_config[0].nat_ip)
}
```

Once you run `terraform apply` and only want to show the outputs, you can run `terraform output` with various options. Without any options, `terraform output` produces the output in human-readable form:

```
$ terraform output
URL_0 = "http://34.171.168.175"
zones-by-servers = [
  "output-0: us-central1-a",
  "output-1: us-central1-b",
  "output-2: us-central1-c",
  "output-3: us-central1-f",
]
...
```

Whereas with the `-json` option, it will produce it in JSON format:

```
$ terraform output -json
{
  "URL_0": {
    "sensitive": false,
    "type": "string",
    "value": "http://34.171.168.175"
  },
  "zones-by-servers": {
```

```
    "sensitive": false,
    "type": [
      "tuple",
      [
        "string",
        "string",
        "string",
        "string"
      ]
    ],
    "value": [
      "output-0: us-central1-a",
      "output-1: us-central1-b",
      "output-2: us-central1-c",
      "output-3: us-central1-f"
    ]
  },
  ...
```

You can specify the name if you want to display only a single value. Using the -raw option does not display any quotes or a newline. This is useful when combining it with other commands, as in the following example:

```
$ curl `terraform output -raw URL_0`
<html><body><p>Hello World!</p></body></html>
```

Outputs are also used to expose information between different Terraform configurations, as seen in the following two chapters.

Tips to develop Terraform code efficiently

> **Note**
>
> The code for this section is under the chap03/error directory in the GitHub repository of this book.

Before we conclude this chapter, we want to introduce two commands that help you develop Terraform code more efficiently. The first command, `terraform fmt`, formats Terraform configuration files so that they follow a consistent format and indentation. Formatting makes the files more readable. However, it can also serve as an initial check, as Terraform reports some syntax errors.

The second command is `terraform validate`. This command performs a syntax check and checks for internal consistency. For example, consider the following file, which contains some incorrect Terraform syntax:

chap02/error/error.tf

```
data "google_compute_zones" "available" {
region = var.region}

data "google_compute_zones" "available" {
region = var.region
}
```

First, run `terraform fmt`, which reports an error stating } must be on a separate line. Fix the error and rerun it. No error is reported, and the file now has a proper indentation. Now, run `terraform validate`. Terraform will report an error as each resource name must be unique. Even though `terraform plan` includes a validation, this command is useful as it does not require you to initialize Terraform; hence, it is slightly faster. It is also commonly used as a separate **continuous integration/continuous deployment (CI/CD)** pipeline step.

When debugging Terraform, setting the log level to get more information can be useful. You can do this by setting the `TF_LOG` environment variable to one of the following log levels: TRACE, DEBUG, INFO, WARN, or ERROR. For more details, please visit `https://www.terraform.io/internals/debugging`.

Give it a try. In Linux, execute the following command:

```
$ export TF_LOG=DEBUG
```

To set the level back to the default, unset the environment variable by running the following command:

```
$ unset TF_LOG
```

Later in this book, we discuss some useful third-party tools that help you debug and improve the quality of your code by performing additional checks such as static code analysis.

Summary

This chapter introduced several new concepts that enable you to write more efficient Terraform code. **Dynamic blocks** are used to write repeatable nested blocks by defining a single block. While Terraform does not have an explicit if-then concept, you can use **conditional expressions** to effectively write if-then structures. Terraform provides several standard built-in functions to create and transform expressions. Data sources refer to resources that are defined outside your Terraform configurations and come in handy at times. Lastly, we discussed output values, which expose Terraform information. You will use these concepts later in the book to develop modules and implement more complex deployments using Terraform.

In the next chapter we will introduce Terraform modules. Modules allow you to reuse blocks of Terraform code, and hence serve a similar purpose as functions in traditional programming languages.

4

Writing Reusable Code Using Modules

One of the main objectives of **Infrastructure as Code** (**IaC**) is to create reusable code using the **Don't Repeat Yourself** (**DRY**) software principle. Andrew Hunt and David Thomas first formulated this principle (*Hunt, Andrew; Thomas, David (1999). The Pragmatic Programmer: From Journeyman to Master (1 ed.). USA: Addison-Wesley. pp. 320. ISBN 978-0201616224*). In essence, it states that we should avoid repeating code.

In functional programming languages, we use functions to keep our code DRY. In Terraform, we use **modules**. In this chapter, we will start by outlining the basic structure of a module and then see how to write flexible modules that will be useful to others in our organization or the community at large. We will then describe how to use private and public Terraform registries to share code in your organization or with the world.

Thus, by the end of this chapter, you will have learned how to write Terraform modules that you (and others) can repeatedly reuse, thus following the DRY principle.

In this chapter, we will cover the following main topics:

- Building modules
- Writing flexible modules
- Sharing modules using buckets and Git repositories
- Using public module repositories

Technical requirements

There are no new technical requirements for this chapter. The code for this chapter is at `https://github.com/PacktPublishing/Terraform-for-Google-Cloud-Essential-Guide/tree/main/chap04`.

Building modules

> **Note**
>
> The code for this section is under the `chap04/local-module` directory in the GitHub repo of this book.

A module in Terraform serves the same purpose as a function in traditional programming languages. A module is a self-contained chunk of code that can be called repeatedly to create cloud infrastructure. Actually, we have already created modules. The Terraform configuration we wrote and executed is known as a **root module**. Modules called from other modules and stored locally are also known as **child modules**. So the root module can call a child module, which can call other modules.

The basic structure of a module is simple. By convention, we have three files: `main.tf`, which contains the main code, `variables.tf`, which defines the variables that need to be passed to the module, and `outputs.tf`, which contains the information passed back to the calling module. Do remember Terraform itself only cares about file extensions, here, `.tf`. Thus, as far as Terraform is concerned, we can name the files anything or even combine them in a single file. However, the convention is to use these three filenames.

So, let us create a module that provides the servers we used as an example. We first define the variables that are to be passed to the module, as shown in the following code:

chap04/local-module/modules/server/variables.tf

```
variable "name" {
  type = string
}
variable "machine_type" {
  type = string
}

variable "zone" {
  type = string
}

variable "static_ip" {
  type = bool
}
```

We then define the resources to be provisioned. Please note that we can define *multiple* resources in a single child module, making them so powerful. In our case, we want to provision a static IP address in addition to a compute engine:

chap04/local-module/modules/server/main.tf

```
resource "google_compute_address" "static" {
  count = var.static_ip ? 1 : 0
  name  = "${var.name}-ipv4-address"
}

resource "google_compute_instance" "this" {
  name          = var.name
  zone          = var.zone
  machine_type  = var.machine_type

  boot_disk {
    initialize_params {
      image = "debian-cloud/debian-11"
    }
  }

  network_interface {
    network = "default"
    dynamic "access_config" {
      for_each = google_compute_address.static
      content {
        nat_ip = access_config.value["address"]
      }
    }
  }

  metadata_startup_script = file("${path.module}/startup.sh")
  tags                    = ["http-server", ]
}
```

Now, let's examine this code in detail. First, we have two resource blocks, one to create the static IP address and another to create the actual server. We now see how useful the trick of using `count` with a conditional expression is. The resource block is applied if `var.static_ip` is set to `true`. If the variable is `false`, the count is zero, and this resource block is not applied.

The resource block to create the compute instance should look familiar except for the startup script line. We need to use the `path.module` variable, which returns the filesystem path where the module is located. If we were to use the relative path like before, using `./`, Terraform would evaluate the path to the current path where it is running, which is the location of the root module.

The third file is the `outputs.tf` file. Remember that we said that the purpose of output values is to expose information. When placed in the root module, the purpose of output values is usually to communicate information to the user. When used in a child module, the objective of an output value is to expose information back to the calling module.

While previously, we didn't pay much attention to the **label** of the output value, in modules, output labels are critical as this is the name to which the output of the modules is referred. Furthermore, only the information defined as an output value can be referenced in the calling module. In our case, we want to expose both the private and public IP address (if it exists). We also mentioned the importance of the `self_link` attribute. Since the main resource we created in this module is the compute instance, it is a good idea to expose the `self_link` attribute to that resource (please note that this is not always the case):

chap04/local-module/modules/server/outputs.tf

```
output "public_ip_address" {
  value = var.static_ip ? google_compute_instance.this.network_
interface.0.access_config.0.nat_ip : null
}

output "private_ip_address" {
  value = google_compute_instance.this.network_
interface.0.network_ip
}

output "self_link" {
  value = google_compute_instance.this.self_link
}
```

Once we have defined our module and placed it in a subdirectory called `modules/server`, we can call it from our root module:

chap04/local-module/main.tf

```
module "server1" {
    source       = "./modules/server"
    name         = "${var.server_name}-1"
    zone         = var.zone
    machine_type = var.machine_type
    static_ip    = true
}
module "server2" {
    source       = "./modules/server"
    name         = "${var.server_name}-2"
    zone         = var.zone
    machine_type = var.machine_type
    static_ip    = false
}

module "server3" {
    source       = "./modules/server"
    name         = "${var.server_name}-3"
    zone         = var.zone
    machine_type = "e2-small"
    static_ip    = true
}
```

Here, we are creating three servers with slightly different variations. We call a module by using the module block followed by a label. The source attribute indicates the location of the module. If it points to a local directory, the module is known as a **local module**. Next, we will specify the arguments that the module is expecting. The `source` argument attribute is mandatory.

All three servers are placed in the zone we defined in `terraform.vars`. We want the first server to have a static IP address and the machine type we defined as the default value. The second server should be similar to the first one except it does not have a static IP address. For the third server, we specify the machine type explicitly.

Writing flexible modules

> **Note**
>
> The code for this section is under the `chap04/flexible-module` directory in the GitHub repo of this book.

Well-written modules should provide a layer of abstraction and be easy to use. It is best to avoid simply writing a module to provide a thin wrapper to existing resource definitions. Modules should provide additional functionality and abstraction.

For example, unless you are an experienced Google Cloud architect, machine types such as N2, E2, and N2D don't have much meaning. For the casual user, it would be much better to provide *T-shirt sizes* for servers, for example, `small`, `medium`, and `large`, and let the module decide which machine type to use.

Using our previous example, we can specify default variable values in the variable declaration blocks of the child module. Any variable with a default value becomes **optional** to the calling module. We declare default values for all variables in the module except the name; thus, all variables except the name become optional.

We also introduce a new `machine_size` variable, which can take the values `small`, `medium`, and `large`. However, we want to ensure that a correct value is passed. If the calling module provides an invalid value, we want to flag it and provide an appropriate error message. For this, Terraform has introduced **Custom Validation Rules**, which you can learn more about at `https://developer.hashicorp.com/terraform/language/values/variables#custom-validation-rules`. A custom validation is a nested block within the variable declaration having `condition` and `error_message` attributes. If the condition is `true`, then the variable value is valid; otherwise, it is not valid, and an error message is produced.

Let's put this into action. First, we modify the variable declaration:

---

chap04/flexible-module/modules/variables.tf

```
variable "name" {
  type = string
}

variable "zone" {
  type    = string
  default = "us-central1-b"
}
```

```
variable "static_ip" {
  type    = bool
  default = true
}


variable "machine_size" {
  type    = string
  default = "small"
  validation {
    condition      = contains(["small", "medium", "large"], var.
machine_size)
    error_message = "The machine size must be one of small,
medium, and large."
  }
}
```

Then, we augment the `main.tf` file in our module. We introduce a new construct, **local values** (learn more about local values here: `https://developer.hashicorp.com/terraform/language/values/locals#local-values`).

In essence, local values are variables that can be used in a module but not outside of it. You declare local values in a `locals` block. The block contains the name of the local value and its value. In our case, we use two local values – `machine_type_mapping` to define the mapping and `machine_type`, which evaluates the actual mapping:

chap04/flexible-module/modules/main.tf

```
locals {
  machine_type_mapping = {
    small  = "e2-micro"
    medium = "e2-medium"
    large  = "n2-standard-2"
  }
  machine_type = local.machine_type_mapping[var.machine_size]
}


resource "google_compute_address" "static" {
  count = var.static_ip ? 1 : 0
```

```
    name  = "${var.name}-ipv4-address"
}

resource "google_compute_instance" "this" {
  name          = var.name
  zone          = var.zone
  machine_type  = local.machine_type

  boot_disk {
    initialize_params {
      image = "debian-cloud/debian-11"
    }
  }

  network_interface {
    network = "default"
    dynamic "access_config" {
      for_each = google_compute_address.static
      content {
        nat_ip = access_config.value["address"]
      }
    }
  }
```

Once we have made the changes to the module, we can then simplify the calling of the child module:

chap04/flexible-module/main.tf

```
module "server1" {
  source        = "./modules/server"
  name          = "${var.server_name}-1"
}

module "server2" {
  source        = "./modules/server"
  name          = "${var.server_name}-2"
  zone          = var.zone
  machine_size  = "medium"
```

```
}

module "server3" {
  source        = "./modules/server"
  name          = "${var.server_name}-3"
  zone          = "us-central1-f"
  machine_size  = "large"
  static_ip     = false
}
```

We only need two lines for `server1`, the source location of the module and the only required attribute, the server name. We specified that the second server should be medium size, and the module mapped the size to the machine instance type. We specified that the third server should be large but without a static (and no public) IP address.

Before we go on, let's look at the zones where each server was placed. Looking at the zones, you can notice that each server is placed in a different zone. We did not specify a zone for the first server, so it took the default value from the child module declaration, which is `us-central1-b`. In the second server, we used the value of the zone variable declared in the root module. We defined the value in the `terraform.tvars` file as `us-central1-c`. For the third server, we defined the value explicitly as `us-central1-f`.

In this section, we described how to make modules more flexible and easier to use so that other people in our organization can use them. Now, let's see how to share modules.

Sharing modules using Google Cloud Storage and Git repositories

> **Note**
>
> The code for this section is under the `chap04/local-module` directory in the GitHub repo of this book.

Modules that are contained within our code are known as local modules. If we want to share a module with other projects or other people, we can store modules in various locations, including **Google Cloud Storage** (**GCS**) and Git repositories. To use a module stored in GCS, we will use the `gcs::` prefix followed by the bucket URL, as in the following example:

```
source = "gcs::https://www.googleapis.com/storage/v1/terraform-
for-gcp/modules/server"
```

We can store the module either as individual files or as a compressed file using zip or gzip. Thus, the following is also valid:

```
source        = "gcs::https://www.googleapis.com/storage/v1/
terraform-for-gcp/modules/server.tar.gz"
```

Please note that you must have the right **Identity and Access Management** (**IAM**) permission to access the files using the bucket URL.

Terraform also supports GitHub and generic Git repositories if you use the `git::` prefix. The advantage of using Git repositories is that it supports versioning. To specify a particular Git version, you need to append the `ref` argument, as in the following example:

```
module "server2" {
  source = "git::https://github.com/PacktPublishing/Terraform-
for-Google-Cloud-Essential-Guide.git//chap04/modules/
server/?ref=2.0.0"
  name        = "${var.server_name}-2"
  zone        = var.zone
  machine_size = "medium"
}
```

For a complete list of source types, please visit `https://developer.hashicorp.com/terraform/language/modules/sources`.

Using public module repositories

> **Note**
> The code for this section is under the `chap04/registry` directory in the GitHub repo of this book.

For Google Cloud, there are two main public module repositories. The official Terraform Registry at `https://registry.terraform.io/browse/modules?provider=google` and Terraform blueprints for Google Cloud at `https://cloud.google.com/docs/terraform/blueprints/terraform-blueprints`.

> **Note**
> Please note that there is some overlap between the two repositories.

While the source code for both the Google blueprints and the Terraform Registry are stored in public GitHub repositories, The Terraform Registry provides some additional functionality. The interface to the Terraform Registry makes it easy to discover the module for our needs. In addition, the Terraform Registry supports versioning. That is, we can put a version constraint when we call a module to ensure that our code uses a specific version we have tested. For example, in the following code, we tested our code with version 5.2.0 and want to ensure that we use this version even if a new module version is available:

chap04/registry/main.tf

```
module "network" {
  source       = "terraform-google-modules/network/google"
  version      = "5.2.0"
  project_id   = var.project_id
  network_name = "my-network"

  subnets = [
    {
      subnet_name   = "us-west1"
      subnet_region = "us-west1"
      subnet_ip     = "10.10.10.0/24"
    },
    {
      subnet_name   = "us-east1"
      subnet_region = "us-east1"
      subnet_ip     = "10.10.20.0/24"
    },
  ]
}

module "deny_ssh_ingress" {
  source        = "terraform-google-modules/network/google//
modules/firewall-rules"
  version      = "5.2.0"
  project_id   = var.project_id
  network_name = module.network.network_name
```

```
  rules = [{
    name                      = "${module.network.network_name}-
deny-ssh-ingress"
    description               = null
    direction                 = "INGRESS"
    priority                  = null
    ranges                    = ["0.0.0.0/0"]
    source_tags               = null
    source_service_accounts = null
    target_tags               = null
    target_service_accounts = null
    deny = [{
      protocol = "tcp"
      ports    = ["22"]
    }]
    allow = []
    log_config = {
      metadata = "INCLUDE_ALL_METADATA"
    }
  }]
}
```

Complex modules often contain submodules, and it can be advantageous to call these submodules directly. Terraform uses a special syntax of `//` to refer to a module within a module. For example, in the configuration file previously, we used the `firewall-rules` submodule to provision a firewall using the following:

```
source        = "terraform-google-modules/network/google//
modules/firewall-rules"
```

Public modules can be useful in two ways. They contain a wide variety of common use cases, from setting up a VPC (learn about it in detail here – `https://github.com/terraform-google-modules/terraform-google-network/tree/master/modules/vpc`) to complex architecture such as configuring a high-availability SAP HANA deployment. Thus, we can use them to quickly provision infrastructure by relying on the works of others. However, they are also convenient for learning from more experienced Terraform developers. As all the code is available on public GitHub repositories, we can look at the actual Terraform code and learn from the best.

Summary

In this chapter, we introduced Terraform modules. Modules are at the heart of IaC as they are the key component to reusing code quickly and efficiently. The structure of a module follows the same structure we have been using to write Terraform code. We declare variables in `variables.tf`, place our main code in `main.tf`, and use the `outputs.tf` file to expose information to the root module.

However, it's important to use modules wisely. A module should *not* be a thin wrapper to existing resource definitions. A well-designed module adds value by providing a layer of abstraction. This can include provisioning multiple resources in a single module and adding organizational patterns and policies. In our albeit simple example, we provisioned not only a server but also a static IP address, and we added a layer of abstraction by providing a mapping of simple server size to instance types.

When you start writing Terraform code, always think about modules. Local modules help to keep your code DRY, particularly when using multiple environments, as we will see in the next chapter.

Lastly, utilize public Terraform module repositories. They provide an excellent starting point whether you use them directly or as a guide to developing your own code.

We started this book by highlighting that one main objective of IaC, besides reuse, is the ability to provision multiple consistent environments, and we will now show this in the next chapter.

5
Managing Environments

The development of every piece of software requires multiple environments. Generally, we use at least three environments – one for development, one for testing, and one for production. However, larger, more complex projects might require additional environments such as training and staging. Supporting multiple environments in a traditional on-premises setting can be costly to create and maintain. The beauty of the cloud is that we have virtually unlimited resources at our disposal. With efficient IaC, we can deploy environments quickly and remove them when they are no longer needed. As we only pay for what we use, we can have as many environments as needed but only pay for them when we actually use them. In this chapter, we will see how to manage multiple environments in Terraform.

This chapter describes the two main methods of managing multiple environments in Terraform – workspaces and directory structure. In particular, we will cover the following topics:

- Google resource hierarchy
- Using workspaces to manage environments
- Using a directory structure to manage environments
- Using remote states
- Using template files

Technical requirements

To follow the code in this project, we require two Google Cloud projects, one to act as the development project and the other as the production project. We can use our existing project as the development project and create a second project for the production environment, or we can create two new ones. If we create a new project, please remember to create the bucket for the state file. If we use a service account (either with a keyfile or with service account impersonation), that service account must have permission to create resources in both projects. Using Cloud Shell for this chapter is easiest as all the permission are set up if you are the owner of both projects.

The code for this chapter can be found here: `https://github.com/PacktPublishing/ Terraform-for-Google-Cloud-Essential-Guide/tree/main/chap05`.

Google resource hierarchy

Before we discuss how to manage environments in Terraform, let's briefly review how to set up environments in Google Cloud. Within Google Cloud, a **project** is a basic container to manage a cloud deployment, including resources, permissions, and billing. When you start with Google Cloud, you generally have one project, then add a second and third project. These projects are entirely independent; that is, they share no IAM permission or resource policy.

As the number of our projects increases, managing these projects, for example, billing and IAM permissions, can become unwieldy. Thus, as we grow our footprint in Google Cloud, it is recommended to set up a **resource hierarchy** (you can read about this more here: `https://cloud.google. com/resource-manager/docs/cloud-platform-resource-hierarchy`) with an **organization** as the root node. This resource hierarchy allows us to organize projects into folders and subfolders. We can then manage permissions on a folder and subfolder level in addition to the project level. For example, we can set IAM permissions and policies at the folder level, which then are inherited down to the project level.

A typical resource hierarchy is shown in *Figure 5.1*. Organizations adopt different folder strategies, but each environment generally resides in its own Google Cloud project. Using separate projects also enables strict separation of namespaces. We can have the same server names in both development and production as they reside in separate projects.

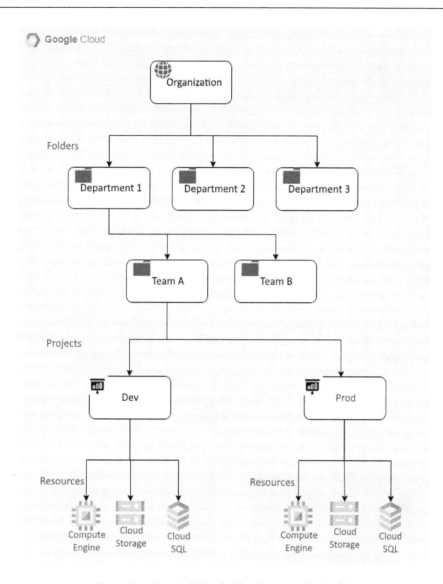

Figure 5.1 – A typical Google Cloud resource hierarchy

For example, in the hierarchy depicted in *Figure 5.1*, we can provision independent resources such as VPCs and virtual machines in both projects – **Dev**, and **Prod**. These resources can even share the same name. We can then allow the development team access to the dev environment in the Dev project and the production team access to the Prod project by setting the appropriate IAM permission on the respective project. However, we can also assign a super user the required IAM permission at the **Team A** folder level, to inherit the permission for both projects. Thus, resource hierarchies provide an ideal way to separate different environments.

Modern software engineering practices dictate that the different environments should be identical or nearly identical except for minor configuration differences. This practice is called dev/prod parity (https://12factor.net/dev-prod-parity). This is to ensure that the application code we developed in a development environment also works in the production environment. IaC enables us to not only create these environments consistently but also provision them quickly when needed and then destroy them when they are not needed in order to save cost.

Within Terraform, there are two established methods to support environments – **workspaces** and **directory structure**.

Using workspaces to manage environments

> **Note**
> The code for this section is under the chap05/workspaces directory in the GitHub repo of this book.

Workspaces allow us to have multiple *independent* state files for a single configuration. Thus, we can have one state file for our development project and a second one for production. By itself, that might appear to be very limited. However, combined with the effective use of variable definitions files (.tfvars) and Google projects, this can be an effective method to manage multiple environments.

Let's see how we can accomplish this. Using the sample code at chap05/workspaces, run terraform init and terraform apply like normal. Then, have a look at the state file using terraform state list:

```
$ terraform init
$ terraform apply
$ terraform state list
```

We can see the three servers and their static IP addresses in the state file.

Next, create a new workspace named prod using the terraform workspace new prod command. The terraform workspace list command shows all the current workspaces and confirms that we are now in the prod workspace.

If we run terraform state list again, Terraform returns an empty list. Terraform created a new state file, and that state is empty:

```
$ terraform workspace new prod
$ terraform workspace list
$ terraform state list
```

Now, run `terraform apply -var project_id=<PRODJECT_ID>` where `<PROJECT_ID>` is the ID of our second project, our production project. Specifying `project_id` on the command line overrides the value provided in `terraform.tfvars`. We can see that it creates identical resources in our production and development projects.

> **Note**
>
> If you run these commands outside of Cloud Shell, you need to set the proper IAM permissions of your Terraform service account in the second project.

The following is a summary of the commands:

```
$ terraform apply -var "project_id=<PROJECT_ID>"
$ terraform state list
```

Now, using the web console, investigate our two projects. We can see that we have created two identical environments, one in each project. That is the power of Terraform combined with the Google Cloud resource hierarchy.

Still in the web console, go to Cloud Storage to view the backend state, which is in our development project. We can see two `.tfstate` files, `default.tfstate` and `prod.tfstate`. Thus, Terraform now manages two independent versions of the state file. You can switch between the two workspaces using `terraform workspace select` and investigate the different state files.

In general, passing variables via the command line is not very efficient. Thus, it is better to create a second variable definition file (`.tfvars`) and pass that on the command line. That is, we edit the `prod.tfvars` file to add the project ID of our production project and run `terraform apply -var-file prod.tfvars`.

Workspaces combined with Google projects can be a powerful tool to manage nearly identical deployments in different environments, but this approach has some limitations. Hence, many organizations use a directory structure to manage different environments.

Using a directory structure to manage environments

> **Note**
>
> The code for this section is under the `chap05/directory-structure` directory in the GitHub repo of this book.

We saw that using workspaces with Google Cloud projects is an easy way to manage nearly identical environments. All we have to do is to create an additional workspace and supply different values in our variable definitions file. However, one of the major limitations of this approach is that the environments must be nearly identical.

Using our example, let's say we want to have two small servers in the development environment, but in the production environment, we want to have two medium and one large server. Provisioning two servers of different sizes is easy, as we can specify different server sizes in the variable definitions file. However, having a third server of a different configuration only in production is more challenging. We could define a combination of conditional expressions and a `count` meta-argument, as follows:

```
count = (terraform.workspace == "prod") ? 1 : 0
```

However, that can get overly complex very quickly. A better approach is to have different subdirectories for each environment and use modules to keep our code DRY. So, if we want to have two environments, our directory structure looks like the following:

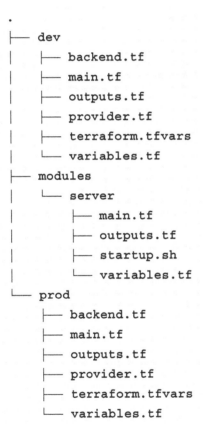

```
.
├── dev
│   ├── backend.tf
│   ├── main.tf
│   ├── outputs.tf
│   ├── provider.tf
│   ├── terraform.tfvars
│   └── variables.tf
├── modules
│   └── server
│       ├── main.tf
│       ├── outputs.tf
│       ├── startup.sh
│       └── variables.tf
└── prod
    ├── backend.tf
    ├── main.tf
    ├── outputs.tf
    ├── provider.tf
    ├── terraform.tfvars
    └── variables.tf
```

We have three subdirectories, dev, prod, and modules. Both dev and prod contain the usual files, including their own backend and variable definitions files. The modules subdirectory contains the configuration files for the server module like before.

So, looking at the two `main.tf` files, we can see how we can define two small servers for dev and three servers of different sizes for prod:

chap05/directory-structure/dev/main.tf

```
module "server1" {
    source       = "../modules/server"
    name         = "${var.server_name}-1"
    machine_size = "small"
    environment  = var.environment
}


module "server2" {
    source       = "../modules/server"
    name         = "${var.server_name}-2"
    machine_size = "small"
    environment  = var.environment
}
```

In `prod/main.tf` we change some variable settings and add one additional module declaration for the third server:

chap05/directory-structure/prod/main.tf

```
module "server1" {
    source       = "../modules/server"
    name         = "${var.server_name}-1"
    machine_size = "medium"
    environment  = var.environment
}


module "server2" {
    source       = "../modules/server"
    name         = "${var.server_name}-2"
    machine_size = "medium"
    environment  = var.environment
}
```

```
module "server3" {
  source        = "../modules/server"
  name          = "${var.server_name}-3"
  machine_size  = "large"
  environment   = var.environment
}
```

With these files in place, we can now run Terraform in each subdirectory specifying the appropriate project ID as an argument:

```
$ cd dev
$ terraform init
$ terraform apply -var project_id=[DEV-PROJECT-ID]
$ cd ../prod
$ terraform init
$ terraform apply -var project_id=[PROD-PROJECT-ID]
```

This structure allows us to have different configurations between the environments yet keep our code DRY. This approach requires the effective use of modules, whether they are stored locally or remotely in Cloud Storage or a repository. When using separate directories, we often need to share state data between the configurations in the different subdirectories. For this, Terraform provides the concept of remote states.

Using remote states

> **Note**
> The code for this section is under the chap05/remote-state directory in the GitHub repo of this book.

Using the directory structure approach provides added flexibility. It is a good approach to decompose complex configurations into smaller, more manageable parts, often called **layers**, when creating complex architectures. Each layer is a logical grouping of resources. For example, let's say we want to provision a database and a set of servers that connect to the database. Furthermore, we have two teams – one responsible for the database and the second managing the servers. In addition, while the database is relatively stable and should be running at all times, we expect the servers to be re-created many times, and we might want to remove the servers over the weekend to save cost.

We can accomplish this goal by creating two layers and placing all configuration files related to the layer in separate subdirectories. That is, we create two subdirectories, `cloud-sql` and `compute-instance`. Each subdirectory has its own configuration files, including the backend and the variable definitions file. Therefore, the file structure looks as follows:

```
.
├── cloud-sql
│   ├── backend.tf
│   ├── main.tf
│   ├── outputs.tf
│   ├── provider.tf
│   ├── terraform.tfvars
│   └── variables.tf
├── compute-instance
│   ├── backend.tf
│   ├── main.tf
│   ├── provider.tf
│   ├── startup.tftpl
│   ├── terraform.tfvars
│   └── variables.tf
```

So, let's first provision the CloudSQL database instance. One of the features of CloudSQL (or, as you might call it – a quirk) is that we cannot reuse the name for up to 1 week after the instance is deleted (`https://cloud.google.com/sql/docs/mysql/create-instance#create-2nd-gen`). Thus, it is common practice to attach a short, unique string to the database name. For this, we use the `random_string` resource in the Terraform `random` provider (`https://registry.terraform.io/providers/hashicorp/random/latest/docs/resources/string`), which is a convenient way to create a random string:

chap05/cloud-sql/main.tf

```
resource "random_string" "this" {
  length  = 4
  special = false
  upper   = false
}
resource "google_sql_database_instance" "main" {
```

```
  name              = "main-instance-${random_string.this.
result}"
  database_version = "POSTGRES_11"
  region            = var.region

  settings {
      tier = "db-f1-micro"
  }
}
```

Now, we run Terraform independently in each subdirectory, starting with `cloud-sql`, but this creates a problem. Since each subdirectory has its own state file, how do we share information from the CloudSQL instance? For example, in order to connect to the database, the compute instance needs to know the connection name of the database that Terraform created. But since the CloudSQL database was configured in a different subdirectory with its own state, the configuration in the `compute-instance` directory does not have access to any of the attributes of `google_sql_database_instance`.

Now, we could use the `google_sql_database_instance` data source (`https://registry. terraform.io/providers/hashicorp/google/latest/docs/data-sources/ sql_database_instance`) using the name of the database, but there is a better way.

The `terraform_remote_state` data source (`https://developer.hashicorp.com/ terraform/language/state/remote-state-data`) enables us to use information from a separate Terraform configuration. That is, in our example, we can use the state information from the `google_sql_database_instance` resource that is defined in the `cloud-sql` directory. As previously, we need to define output values to expose the information we want to share. Since we want to share the `connection_name` value of the database, we expose that value in the `outputs.tf` file:

chap05/remote-state/cloud-sql/outputs.tf

```
output "connection_name" {
  value =   google_sql_database_instance.main.connection_name
}
```

To use that information, we use the `terraform_remote_state` data source in the `compute-instance` directory to retrieve that information. We can then use the connection name using the `data.terraform_remote_state.cloud_sql.outputs.connection_name` expression, as shown in the `data.tf` file that follows:

chap05/ remote-state/compute-instance/data.tf

```
data "terraform_remote_state" "cloud_sql" {
  backend = "gcs"
  config = {
    bucket = "<PROJECT_ID>-tf-state"
    prefix = "chap05/remote-state/cloud-sql"
  }
}


# For Illustration only
output "connection_name" {
  value = data.terraform_remote_state.cloud_sql.outputs.
connection_name
}
```

Now, let's say we want to use the connection name in our startup file. For example, we want to set it as an environment variable that our application code can use to create a connection to the database. How can we pass that information to our startup script?

Using template files

> **Note**
> The code for this section is under the `chap05/remote-state` directory in the GitHub repo of this book.

Terraform provides a built-in function called `templatefile` (read more about it here: `https://developer.hashicorp.com/terraform/language/functions/templatefile`).

This function takes a file that uses Terraform **expressions** and evaluates them. We can use variables, resource attributes, and other expressions in the file, and Terraform evaluates those expressions and replaces them with the values in the files. Let's see this in practice. First, we define a template file. By convention, template files use the `*.tftpl` extension:

chap05/compute-instance/startup.tftpl

```
#! /bin/bash
apt update
apt -y install apache2
cat <<EOF > /var/www/html/index.html
<html><body><p>Hello World!</p>
<p>The CloudSQL connection name is: ${connection_name}</body></
html>
```

During runtime, Terraform evaluates the `data.terraform_remote_state.cloud_sql.outputs.connection_name` expression and replaces it with the value.

Managing Terraform at scale

Before we conclude this chapter, let us look at another aspect of state files. So far, our Terraform files have been manageable as we deployed only a few resources simultaneously. However, even a medium-complexity architecture requires dozens or hundreds of interdependent resources. Using modules, we can reduce this complexity of the Terraform code, but we will still provision many cloud resources with many dependencies. Furthermore, as our use of Terraform grows, we will have teams of several members developing Terraform code simultaneously. Then, managing all resources in a single state file becomes challenging. For example, the team member responsible for the networking might want to change just when another team member is running Terraform to add a virtual machine and hence is prevented from running Terraform simultaneously. Or, the database team wants to use a new feature in the latest provider version that the networking team hasn't been able to test yet.

Thus, it makes sense to break up the state files into separate parts that can be managed independently. When using a directory structure, each subdirectory has its own state file. Having multiple state files brings several advantages with it. First, we can use state files to separate ownership. For example, by dividing all networking, and database-related resources into separate directories, each can have its independent ownership and state files. We can then assign the responsibility of those resources to the networking and database teams, respectively.

Second, we limit the blast radius. With smaller plans, we are less likely to miss destructive changes than if everything is in the same directory and a single state file.

Furthermore, providing separation allows for more granular and safer upgrade paths. As we mentioned, Terraform is a very dynamic environment, with both Terraform and the providers making frequent updates. By separating the state files into independent units, each part can manage upgrades on its own.

Now, managing Terraform at scale for small and large teams is one of the reasons why HashiCorp introduced Terraform Cloud (`https://cloud.hashicorp.com/products/terraform`). Terraform Cloud is a managed service that offers a wide range of features to make it easier and more secure to manage Terraform at scale.

Summary

In this chapter, we introduced the two common methods to support multiple environments in Terraform, workspaces and directory structure. Workspaces create independent state files, which we can use to manage multiple environments – while sufficient for simple deployments, directories are a more flexible way to separate environments in Google Cloud and are generally used to manage environments.

Now that we have covered the fundamentals of Terraform using simple examples, let us build more complex deployments using the techniques you have learned so far. We begin by building a traditional three-tier architecture. Then, we will use a modern serverless architecture using Cloud Run and Redis, before using the public Terraform repository to quickly provision a GKE cluster.

Part 2: Completing the Picture: Provisioning Infrastructure on Google Cloud

In this part of the book, we apply the concepts introduced in the first part of the book to construct three complete architectures using Terraform. We start with a traditional three-tier architecture. We show how to use layers effectively and how to expose state information between the layers. In *Chapter 7*, we deploy a modern cloud-native architecture using only serverless services. One of the services, Google Cloud Run, blurs the line between infrastructure and application. We contrast using Terraform to deploy Cloud Run services to using gcloud. In this part's last chapter, we use modules from the public Terraform registry to deploy a GKE cluster in two environments (development and production) by only varying variable assignments.

After reading this part, you will have deployed three very different architectures using Terraform while also gaining a deeper understanding and appreciation of the power of Terraform.

This part of the book comprises the following chapters:

- *Chapter 6, Deploying a Traditional Three-Tier Architecture*
- *Chapter 7, Deploying a Cloud-Native Architecture Using Cloud Run*
- *Chapter 8, Deploying GKE Using Public Modules*

Deploying a Traditional Three-Tier Architecture

We have covered the fundamentals of Terraform for Google Cloud using simple examples so far in this book. We will apply those fundamentals in the next three chapters to build complete architectures. In this chapter, we will build a *traditional* three-tier architecture with virtual machines for the application layer and Cloud SQL for the database layer. In the next chapter, we will create a completely serverless architecture using Cloud Run and Redis. In *Chapter 8, Deploying GKE Using Public Modules*, we will then provision a Google Kubernetes Engine cluster using public repositories.

In this chapter, we will cover the following topics:

- Laying the foundation
- Provisioning a complete database using Cloud SQL
- Deploying a MIG and global load balancer

Technical requirements

We recommend creating a fresh new Google Cloud project for this sample code. As before, we need to create the bucket for the remote Terraform state file outside of Terraform using the web console or a `gcloud` command. The code in the GitHub repository – `https://github.com/PacktPublishing/Terraform-for-Google-Cloud-Essential-Guide/tree/main/chap06` – will work for a new project. Just remember to run `terraform destroy` afterward, as the cloud resources will incur costs.

If you use a service account for Terraform, you need to set the appropriate IAM permission, including **Project IAM Admin** and **Secret Manager Admin** permissions.

Overview

Some may not consider a traditional three-tier architecture consisting of a load balancer, a **managed instance group** (**MIG**) of virtual machines as the application layer, and Cloud SQL for the database tier a cloud-native architecture. Yet, it is still a pervasive architecture and a good starting point to apply the concepts we have learned about so far. *Figure 6.1* shows the diagram of the architecture that we will provision in this chapter:

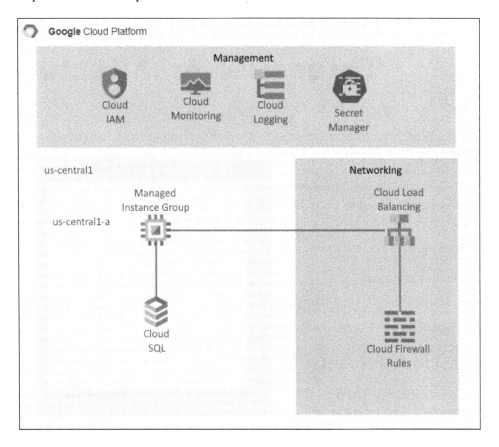

Figure 6.1 – Three-tier architecture

Following Google Cloud best practices, we use a custom VPC with minimal subnets and firewall rules. As we are catering to HTTP traffic, we are utilizing a global load balancer, which acts as the entry point and direct traffic to virtual machines that host our application code.

We deploy the virtual machines (compute engine) in a MIG to allow scaling. For the database tier, we create a Cloud SQL instance and use Secret Manager to store the connection information, which the application code can access to connect to the database.

As described in the previous chapter, we use a layered approach to provision the resources. Each layer, or subdirectory, has its own state file, and we use the `terraform_remote_state` **data source** to expose the state information of the different layers. In the first layer, we enable the required APIs and configure the custom VPC, along with the appropriate firewall rules. Next, we provision the database instance, the database, and the database user. Finally, we provision the MIG and the load balancer.

> **Note**
>
> Please note that we made some simplifications to reduce the cost and complexity of the sample code. These include provisioning the database in a single zone with a public IP address and using HTTP instead of HTTPS to connect to our application.

Laying the foundation

> **Note**
>
> The code for this section is under the `chap06/foundation` directory in the GitHub repository of this book. Please note that we divided the code into small files for readability purposes.

In the first layer, we set the foundation for this architecture. First, we enable the appropriate APIs using the `google_project_service` resource. For this project, we require the following APIs:

- Cloud Resource Manager
- Compute Engine
- Identity and Access Management
- Secret Manager API

The `google_project_service` resource has an optional argument, `disable_on_destroy`, which is set to `true` by default. It is usually better to set it to `false`, which mimics the behavior when we enable APIs using the web console.

As we are creating multiple `google_project_service` resources, this is an ideal opportunity to use the `for_each` meta-argument. `for_each` requires a set – we use the `toset()` function which converts a list to a set. This function is useful in conjunction with the `for_each` meta-argument, as `toset()` removes any duplicates and discards the ordering.

chap06/foundation/project-services.tf

```
resource "google_project_service" "this" {
  for_each        = toset(var.services)
  service         = "${each.key}.googleapis.com"
```

```
    disable_on_destroy = false
}
```

In this layer, we also provision the VPC, including the firewall rules. As we only use one region, we can set up a simple VPC with only one subnet. Following the best security protocols, we provision stringent firewall rules. The global load balancer handles all inbound traffic, so we do not need to provision any firewall rule to allow `http` inbound traffic. However, the load balancer requires a firewall rule to allow ingress for the health checks (for more details, refer to – `https://cloud.google.com/load-balancing/docs/health-checks#firewall_rules`).

Now, this firewall rule allows ingress from specific IP ranges (`35.191.0.0/16` and `130.211.0.0/22`). We could hardcode those IP ranges as in the documentation. However, using Terraform, we can use a data source to retrieve those IP ranges dynamically. The `google_netblock_ip_ranges` (`https://registry.terraform.io/providers/hashicorp/google/latest/docs/data-sources/netblock_ip_ranges`) data source retrieves the unique IP ranges used by Google Cloud, and we can use it to retrieve the IP ranges for the health checkers.

During development, we want to provide `ssh` access to the virtual machines. Still, we want to restrict access to authorized users only, and we use Google Cloud **Identity-Aware Proxy** (**IAP**) to do so. If you are not aware of IAP, be sure to check out the documentation at `https://cloud.google.com/iap`. IAP is part of the Google Cloud security framework and enables virtual machines to access without the need for a VPN or bastion host.

To allow access to virtual machines using IAP, we need to set up a firewall rule to allow `ssh` access from a specific set of source IP ranges. We can use the `google_netblock_ip_ranges` data source to retrieve those specific IP ranges used in the firewall rule:

chap06/foundation/data.tf

```
data "google_netblock_ip_ranges" "iap_forwarders" {
  range_type = "iap-forwarders"
}
data "google_netblock_ip_ranges" "health_checkers" {
  range_type = "health-checkers"
}
```

Thus, we use two `google_netblock_ip_ranges` data sources to retrieve the two IP ranges and then use them to configure the firewall rules, shown as follows:

chap06/foundation/firewall.tf

```
resource "google_compute_firewall" "allow_iap" {
  name    = "${local.network_name}-allow-iap"
```

```
   network = local.network_name

   allow {
     protocol = "tcp"
     ports    = ["22"]
   }

   source_ranges = data.google_netblock_ip_ranges.iap_
forwarders.cidr_blocks_ipv4
   target_tags   = ["allow-iap"]
}

resource "google_compute_firewall" "allow_health_check" {
   name    = "${local.network_name}-allow-health-check"
   network = local.network_name
   allow {
     protocol = "tcp"
     ports    = ["80"]
   }

   source_ranges = data.google_netblock_ip_ranges.health_
checkers.cidr_blocks_ipv4
   target_tags   = ["allow-health-check"]
}
```

Following the security principle of least privilege, the virtual machines in the instance group use a dedicated service account that only has the required permission to complete its tasks. In this case, we require the `cloudsql.client` and `secretmanager.secretAccessor` permissions, so we need to create a service account and assign the appropriate roles. Terraform provides two resources to assign IAM roles, `google_project_iam_binding` and `google_project_iam_member` (read about them in detail here – `https://registry.terraform.io/providers/ hashicorp/google/latest/docs/resources/google_project_iam`).

The main difference between the two resources is that the former is **authoritative**, whereas the latter is **non-authoritative**. That is, `google_project_iam_binding` overwrites any other IAM permission, whereas `google_project_iam_member` is additive, which preserves any existing IAM permission. In general, it is better to use `google_project_iam_member` or the use IAM module from Google (read more about the best practices here – `https://cloud.google.com/docs/terraform/best-practices-for-terraform#iam`):

chap06/foundation/sa.tf

```
resource "google_service_account" "this" {
  account_id   = var.sa_name
  display_name = "${var.sa_name} Service Account"
}

resource "google_project_iam_member" "this" {
  project = var.project_id
  count   = length(var.roles)
  role    = "roles/${var.roles[count.index]}"
  member  = "serviceAccount:${google_service_account.this.
email}"
}
```

Now that we have enabled all the required APIs, set up the VPC, including the firewall rules, and provisioned the service account, we can proceed to the second layer, creating the database and the database users.

If you have created a new project for this exercise, we recommend manually removing the default VPC network. Note that we only allow `ssh` access via IAP – as in, the specific IAP ports, and not via `0.0.0.0/0` as in the default VPC. This is a recommended security practice in Google Cloud.

Provisioning the database

> **Note**
> The code for this section is in the `chap06/database` directory in the GitHub repository of this book.

In the previous chapter, we provisioned a Cloud SQL instance to demonstrate the use of a remote state. We will now provision a complete database along with a user and password. Following good security practices, we use **Google Cloud Secret Manager** to securely store the passwords to retrieve them in the application layer.

> **Note**
> While Google Cloud Secret Manager stores the secret in an encrypted fashion, the secret remains in plaintext in the Terraform state file, so take extra care to protect the state file from unwarranted access.

So, first, we generate the root and user password using the `random_password` Terraform resource. Next, we store the generated passwords in the secret manager. We need to use two resources each – `google_secret_manager_secret` to provision the secret and `google_secret_manager_secret_version` to store the actual password:

chap06/database/secrets.tf

```
resource "random_password" "root" {
  length  = 12
  special = false
}

resource "google_secret_manager_secret" "root_pw" {
  secret_id = "db-root-pw"
  replication {
    automatic = true
  }
}

resource "google_secret_manager_secret_version" "root_pw_version" {
  secret      = google_secret_manager_secret.root_pw.id
  secret_data = random_password.root.result
}

resource "random_password" "user" {
  length  = 8
  special = false
}

resource "google_secret_manager_secret" "user_pw" {
  secret_id = "db-user-pw"
  replication {
```

```
    automatic = true
  }
}


resource "google_secret_manager_secret_version" "user_pw_
version" {
  secret       = google_secret_manager_secret.user_pw.id
  secret_data = random_password.user.result
}
```

Once we have created and stored the passwords, we can create the database instance, database, and
database user. We used the remote state in the previous chapter to pass the connection name to the
application layer. However, we can also store the connection name in the secret manager and pass it
as a secret to the application code:

chap06/database/main.tf

```
resource "random_string" "this" {
  length  = 4
  upper   = false
  special = false
}


resource "google_sql_database_instance" "this" {
  name            = "${var.db_settings.instance_name}-
${random_string.this.result}"
  database_version = var.db_settings.database_version
  region          = var.region
  root_password   = random_password.root.result

  settings {
    tier = var.db_settings.database_tier
  }
  deletion_protection = false
}


resource "google_sql_database" "this" {
  name      = var.db_settings.db_name
```

```
    instance = google_sql_database_instance.this.name
}

resource "google_sql_user" "sql" {
    name     = var.db_settings.user_name
    instance = google_sql_database_instance.this.name
    password = random_password.user.result
}

resource "google_secret_manager_secret" "connection_name" {
    secret_id = "connection-name"
    replication {
        automatic = true
    }
}

resource "google_secret_manager_secret_version" "connection_
name" {
    secret      = google_secret_manager_secret.connection_name.id
    secret_data = google_sql_database_instance.this.connection_
name
}
```

Please note that to reduce the Terraform code's complexity, we configure the Cloud SQL instance with a public IP address and access it via the SQL proxy (`https://cloud.google.com/sql/docs/mysql/sql-proxy`) in our sample code. Please see the documentation at `https://cloud.google.com/sql/docs/mysql/connect-overview` for the various options to connect to Cloud SQL.

Now that we have completed the database provisioning, we can proceed to the last layer of provisioning the load balancer and the MIG.

Provisioning a MIG and global load balancer

> **Note**
>
> The code for this section is under the `chap06/main` directory in the GitHub repository of this book.

To create a MIG, we first create an **instance template**, and then the MIG, which uses the instance template. The instance group is analogous to creating a virtual machine. Please note that we specify the service account we created and set the scopes to `cloud-platform`. That follows Google Cloud best practices: `https://cloud.google.com/compute/docs/access/service-accounts#scopes_best_practice`.

Now, here, we can put the `create_before_destroy` **life cycle** rule to good use. Let's say we want to change the instance template by, for example, changing the startup script. Usually, Terraform destroys the `google_compute_instance_template` resource before applying the change and creating a new resource. However, Google Cloud won't let us destroy `google_compute_instance_template` because the MIG still uses it. Hence, we use the `create_before_destroy` life cycle meta-argument to instruct Terraform to create a new template, apply that to the MIG, and only then destroy the old one. However, there is one more thing we need to do. If we declare a fixed name for the instance template, the `create_before_destroy` life cycle would report a naming conflict, as it would try to create a second instance template with the same name. Hence, instead of specifying a name for `google_compute_instance_template`, we use the `name_prefix` attribute shown as follows:

chap06/main/mig.tf

```
resource "google_compute_instance_template" "this" {
  name_prefix   = var.mig.instance_template_name_prefix
  region        = var.region
  machine_type  = var.mig.machine_type

  disk {
    source_image = var.mig.source_image
  }

  network_interface {
    subnetwork = data.terraform_remote_state.foundation.
outputs.subnetwork_self_links["iowa"]
    access_config {
      // Ephemeral public IP
    }
  }

  metadata_startup_script = file("startup.sh")
```

```
  tags = [
    "allow-iap",
    "allow-health-check"
  ]
  service_account {
    email   = data.terraform_remote_state.foundation.outputs.
service_account_email
    scopes = ["cloud-platform"]
  }

  lifecycle {
    create_before_destroy = true
  }
}
```

As we want our instance group to be **high availability** (**HA**), we create a regional MIG. In this example, we want to apply updates automatically, so we choose **proactive** updates (https://cloud.google.com/compute/docs/instance-groups/rolling-out-updates-to-managed-instance-groups#type). Thus, as soon as a change is detected in the instance template, Google Cloud updates the virtual machines:

chap06/main/mig.tf

```
resource "google_compute_region_instance_group_manager" "this"
{
  name               = var.mig.mig_name
  region             = var.region
  base_instance_name = var.mig.mig_base_instance_name
  target_size        = var.mig.target_size

  version {
    instance_template = google_compute_instance_template.this.
id
  }

  named_port {
    name = "http"
    port = 80
```

```
  }

  update_policy {
    type              = "PROACTIVE"
    minimal_action    = "REPLACE"
    max_surge_fixed   = 3
  }
}
```

Defining the global load balancer is a four-step process analogous to creating it using the web console. First, we need to create a frontend configuration using the google_compute_global_ forwarding_rule resource. Next, we need to define a backend service (google_compute_ backend_service), along with a health check (google_compute_health_check). Then, lastly, we create the path rules using the google_compute_url_map resource:

chap06/main/lb.tf

```
resource "google_compute_global_forwarding_rule" "this" {
  name                    = var.load_balancer.forward_rule_name
  ip_protocol             = "TCP"
  load_balancing_scheme   = "EXTERNAL"
  port_range              = "80"
  target                  = google_compute_target_http_proxy.
this.self_link
}

resource "google_compute_health_check" "this" {
  name = "http-health-check"
  http_health_check {
    port = 80
  }
}

resource "google_compute_backend_service" "this" {
  name                    = var.load_balancer.backend_service_
name
  health_checks           = [google_compute_health_check.this.
self_link]
```

```
  load_balancing_scheme = "EXTERNAL"

  backend {
    balancing_mode = "UTILIZATION"
    group          = google_compute_region_instance_group_
manager.this.instance_group
  }
}

resource "google_compute_url_map" "this" {
  name            = var.load_balancer.url_map_name
  default_service = google_compute_backend_service.this.self_
link
}

resource "google_compute_target_http_proxy" "this" {
  name    = var.load_balancer.target_proxy_name
  url_map = google_compute_url_map.this.self_link
}
```

Now, we can run Terraform and then access the resulting website using the IP address shown in the output.

> **Note**
>
> Please note that the global load balancer takes a few minutes to become fully active.

We included some sample code to demonstrate the use of accessing the secret manager during startup time, and the use of an SQL proxy (https://cloud.google.com/sql/docs/mysql/sql-proxy) to use the access database. Thus, we can ssh into the instance from the web console and cut and paste the code shown into the command line of your ssh session to connect to the database. We can retrieve the password using the web console or the following command:

```
$ gcloud secrets versions access latest --secret="db-user-pw"
```

We see that we can successfully connect to the database without any hardcoded connection information. Please note that this is for demonstration purposes only.

Now, let's make a change in the `startup.sh` file by changing the version number in the HTML part from V1.0 to V2.0, and run Terraform again. Terraform replaces `google_compute_instance_template` but creates the new instance template first before destroying the existing one due to the life cycle rule. If we go into the web console, we can observe the changes. The number of virtual machines temporarily increases to six instances.

Summary

In this chapter, we applied the concepts learned in the previous chapters. We used a layered approach to deploy a traditional three-tier architecture. In the first layer, we applied the `for_each` meta-attribute to efficiently enable multiple project services using only four lines of code. We also used a **data source** to retrieve two special IP address ranges from Google Cloud.

In the second layer, we created a complete database. We used Terraform to generate passwords and store them in Google Cloud Secret Manager so the application layer could retrieve them. In the third layer, we used the life cycle **meta-attribute** to deploy new instance templates. We also showed how we can store sensitive information in the secret manager that the application code can retrieve.

Now that we have used Terraform to provision a traditional architecture, we will deploy a modern, highly scalable cloud architecture using only serverless cloud resources in the next chapter.

7

Deploying a Cloud-Native Architecture Using Cloud Run

In the previous chapter, we applied concepts we covered in this book's first part to create a *traditional* three-tier architecture. In this chapter, we will deploy a cloud-native architecture using only managed Google Cloud services. The central component of this architecture is **Cloud Run** (`https://cloud.google.com/run`), Google Cloud's managed service to deploy containers in a serverless fashion.

Again, we will use a layered approach while reusing some of the code from the previous chapter. Then, we will show how to provision a flexible load balancer that serves static content from Cloud Storage and can accommodate any Cloud Run service without any changes to the load balancer.

We will also show two contrasting methods to deploy a Cloud Run service – one using Terraform, and a second one using a `gcloud` command – so that you can decide which method works better in your environment.

In this chapter, we're going to cover the following main topics:

- Provisioning Redis and connecting it via a VPC connector
- Using Terraform to configure a flexible load balancer for Cloud Run
- Using Terraform to provision Cloud Run services
- To Terraform or not to Terraform

Technical requirements

If you ran `terraform destroy` in the project from the previous chapter, you can reuse it, or you can create a new project. The code in this book's GitHub repository (`https://github.com/PacktPublishing/Terraform-for-Google-Cloud-Essential-Guide/tree/main/chap07`) works either way. You should destroy the project afterwards to save costs. If you use a service account for Terraform, ensure you have the appropriate IAM permissions, including Secret Manager Admin and Cloud Run Admin Permissions.

This chapter assumes you have a basic knowledge of Docker containers and Cloud Run (`https://cloud.google.com/run`). If you are new to Cloud Run, we suggest that you complete one of the many examples in the Cloud Run Quickstarts (`https://cloud.google.com/run/docs/quickstarts`).

Overview

Managed Cloud Run is a highly efficient and scalable way to run stateless containers in Google Cloud. When combining it with other managed services such as the global load balancer and Google Cloud's managed database services, whether Cloud SQL or Memory Store, Cloud Run deploys a scalable and very cost-effective architecture in minutes.

Figure 7.1 is a graphical representation of the architecture that we will provision. Traffic enters through a **global load balancer**. We configure the load balancer to serve static content, including the home page from **Cloud Storage**, but Cloud Run serves the dynamic content. The global load balancer is a layer 7 load balancer that supports path-based routing. That means we can configure it so that any URL with the `/api` prefix is directed to Cloud Run. Furthermore, we can configure the load balancer to dynamically map the URL to the name of the Cloud Run service. The URL with the `/api/<service>` prefix automatically maps to the Cloud Run service with that name. For example, `http://www.example.com/api/hello` is served by the Cloud Run service called `hello`, whereas `http://www.example.com/api/view` is served by the Cloud Run `view` service. This makes it very flexible as we can add new Cloud Run services and have them served immediately by the load balancer without any configuration changes.

In this example, we will use Redis as a managed database to store any persistent data, though we could utilize other database services, such as Cloud SQL or Firestore:

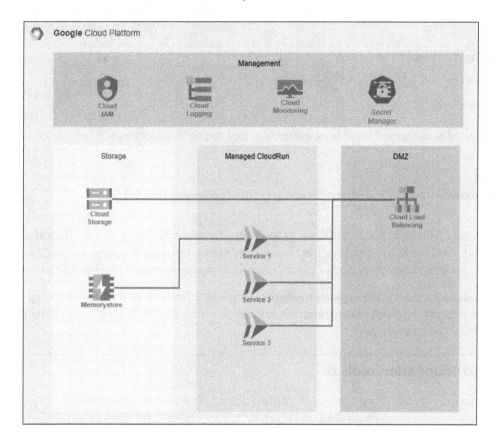

Figure 7.1 – Cloud Run architecture

Again, we are using a layered approach to provision this architecture. In the first layer, we build the VPC and the database. We create the load balancer and the Cloud Run services in the second layer.

Provisioning Redis and connecting it via a VPC connector

> **Note**
> The code for this section can be found in the chap07/foundation directory in this book's GitHub repository.

Similar to what we did in the previous chapter, we will start by building the foundation. This architecture requires several project services, a service account, and a VPC with one subnet. As we used the same setup in the previous chapter, we can simply reuse the code from the previous chapter by copying the following files:

- `project-services.tf`
- `sa.tf`
- `vpc.tf`

We only need to change our variable assignments in `terraform.tfvars`.

> **Note**
>
> Of course, it would be even more efficient to create modules and then use them.

Provisioning a basic Redis instance in Google Cloud using Terraform only requires a few lines of code. However, for a Cloud Run service to connect to Redis, we need to create a VPC connector (`https://cloud.google.com/vpc/docs/configure-serverless-vpc-access`).

Here is one of the cases where we want to use the Google Beta provider. At the time of writing this book, the subnet argument was only available in the Beta version. Hence, we are explicitly specifying the `google-beta` provider:

chap07/foundation/redis.tf

```
resource "google_vpc_access_connector" "this" {
  provider = google-beta
  name      = var.vpc_connector_name
  region    = var.region
  subnet {
    name        = var.subnets[0].name
  }
}

resource "google_redis_instance" "this" {
  name               = "redis"
  memory_size_gb     = 1
  tier               = "BASIC"
  region             = var.region
  authorized_network = google_compute_network.this.self_link
```

```
}
resource "google_secret_manager_secret" "redis_ip" {
  secret_id  = "redis-ip"
  replication {
    automatic = true
  }
}
resource "google_secret_manager_secret" "redis_ip" {
  depends_on = [google_project_service.this["secretmanager"]]
  secret_id  = "redis-ip"
  replication {
    automatic = true
  }
}
```

As we did previously, we store the connection information – in this case, the IP address of the Redis instance – in the secret manager so that we can easily pass the value to Cloud Run.

Using Terraform to configure a flexible load balancer for Cloud Run

> **Note**
> The code for this section can be found in the chap07/main directory in this book's GitHub repository.

In the previous chapter, we provisioned a global load balancer using Terraform. In this architecture, we will expand on it by making it more flexible – all static assets will be served from Cloud Storage, whereas all dynamic traffic will be served from Cloud Run.

Google Cloud Storage is a very cost-effective way to host static assets for web applications, such as images, CSS files, and static HTML pages. Two configurations are required to use a bucket as a website. First, we need to assign specialty pages such as the default page and notFoundpage (https://cloud.google.com/storage/docs/hosting-static-website#specialty-pages).

Second, as our website is open to the public, we need to make the bucket publicly accessible by using the `google_storage_bucket_iam_binding` resource. We will also use Terraform to upload the actual specialty pages and a sample image, as shown in the following code:

chap06/main/website.tf

```
resource "google_storage_bucket" "static" {
  name                        = "${var.project_id}-static"
  location                    = var.region
  uniform_bucket_level_access = true

  website {
    main_page_suffix = "index.html"
    not_found_page   = "404.html"
  }
}

resource "google_storage_bucket_iam_binding" "binding" {
  bucket  = google_storage_bucket.static.name
  role    = "roles/storage.objectViewer"
  members = ["allUsers", ]
}
resource "google_storage_bucket_object" "index" {
  name          = "index.html"
  source        = "../static/index.html"
  bucket        = google_storage_bucket.static.name
  cache_control = "no-store"
}
...
```

The setup of the global load balancer is similar to the one in the previous chapter, with a few additions. First, we must configure a serverless **Network Endpoint Group** (NEG) (`https://cloud.google.com/load-balancing/docs/negs/serverless-neg-concepts`) to use a serverless service such as Cloud Run. Then, we must set up a **backend service** that points to that NEG. A particularly useful feature of a serverless NEG is the concept of a URL mask. (`https://cloud.google.com/load-balancing/docs/negs/serverless-neg-concepts#url_masks`).

A URL mask maps the URL path to the service without specifying the actual service name. For example, we can define a URL mask of `/api/<service>`. Thus, any call on our website with the `/api` prefix will map to the Cloud Run service of that name. For example, `http://example.com/api/hello` maps to the Cloud Run `hello` service, whereas `http://example.com/api/login` maps to the Cloud Run `login` service. This feature is handy, particularly for an application that utilizes microservices, as shown here:

chap06/main/load-balancer.tf

```
resource "google_compute_region_network_endpoint_group" "api" {
  name                  = "cloud-run"
  network_endpoint_type = "SERVERLESS"
  region                = var.region
  cloud_run {
    url_mask = "/api/<service>"
  }
}


resource "google_compute_backend_service" "api" {
  name                  = "cloud-run"
  load_balancing_scheme = "EXTERNAL"
  port_name             = "http"

  backend {
    group                = google_compute_region_network_endpoint_
group.api.self_link
  }
}
```

At this point, we have configured the load balancer, and we can test it by accessing static assets.

> **Note**
> The load balancer takes a few minutes to become fully operational after being provisioned.

However, we have not deployed any Cloud Run Services yet. Remember that we discussed the overlap between **Infrastructure as Code** (**IaC**) and configuration management in *Chapter 1, Getting Started with Terraform on Google Cloud.* Now, Cloud Run is an interesting managed service. It deploys application code in the form of containers in seconds. So, is Cloud Run infrastructure, or is it application code? Should we use Terraform to deploy Cloud Run, or is it easier to use another tool to deploy Cloud Run services? The answer, of course, is: it depends. First, we will use Terraform to provision two Cloud Run services, and then we will use the CLI (`gcloud`) to deploy the same Cloud Run services. Thus, you can compare the two methods and decide which will work better in your environment.

Using Terraform to provision Cloud Run services

In our example, we will deploy two Cloud Run services. The first one is a simple `Hello` example. The second service accesses the Redis database. We will include the code for both services for your reference so that you can build your own container images. The sample code uses container images from a public container repository.

We want the Cloud Run service to be publicly accessible – that is, not require any authentication. For enhanced security, we will allow the Cloud Run services to ingress only via the load balancer and use the service account we provisioned in the foundation layer.

First, let's have a look at how we deploy the `hello` service. First, we must provision the Cloud Run service using the `google_cloud_run_service` resource. We need to specify the container source and the service account name. To restrict the ingress restriction, we need to add an annotation, as follows:

chap06/main/cloudrun.tf

```
resource "google_cloud_run_service" "hello" {
  name     = "hello"
  location = var.region
  metadata {
    annotations = {
      "run.googleapis.com/ingress" = "internal-and-cloud-load-
balancing"
    }
  }


  template {
    spec {
      containers {
        image = var.container_images.hello
      }
      service_account_name = data.terraform_remote_state.
foundation.outputs.service_account_email
```

```
      }
    }
  }
  resource "google_cloud_run_service_iam_binding" "hello_world" {
    location = google_cloud_run_service.hello_world.location
    service  = google_cloud_run_service.hello_world.name
    role     = "roles/run.invoker"
    members = [
      "allUsers",
    ]
  }
```

Now, by default, Cloud Run services require authentication. We need to set the appropriate IAM service policy to allow public access. There are several ways to set or update the IAM policy for a Cloud Run service (`https://registry.terraform.io/providers/hashicorp/google/latest/docs/resources/cloud_run_service_iam`). We will choose the **authoritative** method of using the `google_cloud_run_service_iam_binding` resource. Authoritative means that it will replace the current IAM policy if it exists. We must set the role of `roles/run.invoker`, which sets the permission to invoke a Cloud Run service and use `allUsers` as a member. `allUsers` is a special identifier in Google Cloud that denotes any user – that is, the Cloud Run service is open to the public.

Now that we have provisioned the simple `hello` service, let's focus on the Cloud Run service that accesses the Redis instance we created in the foundation. The Redis service requires two additions. We want to pass the Redis IP that we stored in the secret manager, and we need to specify that the Cloud Run service uses the VPC connector.

To specify the VPC connector, we need to add two annotations to our template. To retrieve the secret from the secret manager, we can use a special block called `value_from`, which is nested in the env block. The `value_from` block specifies to dynamically retrieve the value of the secret stored when the Cloud Run service is provisioned and passes it as an environment variable to the container. Please note that Terraform only passes the secret's name, not the secret's actual value. The secret's value – the actual password – is retrieved dynamically when the container is created, as can be seen in the following code:

chap06/main/cloudrun.tf

```
resource "google_cloud_run_service" "redis" {
  name = "redis"

  location = var.region
```

```
  metadata {
    annotations = {
      "run.googleapis.com/ingress" = "internal-and-cloud-load-
balancing"
    }
  }
  template {
    metadata {
      annotations = {
        "run.googleapis.com/vpc-access-connector" = var.vpc_
connector_name
        "run.googleapis.com/vpc-access-egress"    = "private-
ranges-only"
      }
    }
    spec {
      containers {
        image = var.container_images.redis
        env {
          name = "REDIS_IP"
          value_from {
            secret_key_ref {
              name = data.terraform_remote_state.foundation.
outputs.redis_ip_secret_id
              key  = "latest"
            }
          }
        }
      }
      service_account_name = data.terraform_remote_state.
foundation.outputs.service_account_email
    }
  }
}

resource "google_cloud_run_service_iam_binding" "redis" {
  location = google_cloud_run_service.redis.location
```

```
  service   = google_cloud_run_service.redis.name
  role      = "roles/run.invoker"
  members = [
    "allUsers",
  ]
}
```

> **Note**
>
> If you get an IAM policy error, please ensure that your Terraform service account has the Cloud Run Admin role.

As you can see, the preceding code is not trivial and requires much data to be passed as metadata. So, the question is – should we use Terraform in this case or are other, better alternatives?

To Terraform or not to Terraform

As we mentioned earlier, Cloud Run is a fully managed Google Cloud service that blurs the line between infrastructure and application code. Terraform is designed to provision cloud infrastructure. For example, if a developer updates the code of the Cloud Run service container image and a new image is built, the infrastructure – that is, the Cloud Run service – has not changed. Thus, upon rerunning Terraform, it does not detect any difference and does not deploy a new version of the Cloud Run service. We could explicitly update the version of the container image every time we update the code, then specify the version as part of the container image, or we can use something else to deploy Cloud Run services.

For example, we can use the Google Cloud CLI. (You can read more about it here: `https://cloud.google.com/sdk/gcloud/reference/run/deploy`.) The following `gcloud` commands are equivalent to the Terraform code in the `cloudrun.tf` file:

```
$ export SERVICE_ACCOUNT=`gcloud iam service-accounts list \
--format="value(email)"  --filter=name:cloudrun`

$ gcloud run deploy hello  --region us-central1   \
  --image gcr.io/terraform-for-gcp/helloworld:latest \
  --platform managed  --allow-unauthenticated  \
  --service-account $SERVICE_ACCOUNT \
  --ingress internal-and-cloud-load-balancing
```

```
$ gcloud run deploy redis  --region us-central1    \
  --image gcr.io/terraform-for-gcp/redis:latest \
  --platform managed  --allow-unauthenticated  \
  --service-account $SERVICE_ACCOUNT \
  --ingress internal-and-cloud-load-balancing \
   --vpc-connector vpccon \
  --update-secrets=REDIS_IP=redis-ip:latest \
 --ingress internal-and-cloud-load-balancing
```

There is a one-to-one relationship between the gcloud command and the Terraform resources. You can decide which method works best for you: Terraform or gcloud.

We mentioned earlier that we configured the load balancer to be flexible. Thus, we can add a Cloud Run service and have it immediately accessible through the load balancer. For example, the following gcloud command deploys the sample Cloud Run container:

```
$ gcloud run deploy my-hello --region us-central1    \
 --image us-docker.pkg.dev/cloudrun/container/hello \
 --platform managed --allow-unauthenticated \
 --service-account $SERVICE_ACCOUNT \
 --ingress internal-and-cloud-load-balancing
```

Once it has been deployed, it is accessible through http://<ip-address>/api/my-hello.

Thus, in this architecture, you can easily use Cloud Run to deploy additional microservices, which the load balancer can service without any changes. Hence, developers can add microservices by simply developing code, deploying it into a container image, and then using a single gcloud command to add it to the application.

Summary

In this chapter, we deployed a modern, serverless architecture using Terraform. We reused existing code from the previous chapter so that we could build a foundation with new variable assignments and a few lines of additional Terraform code to provision the Redis database and the VPC connector.

Then, we set up a static website and a flexible global load balancer to map a URL to the corresponding Cloud Run service. Lastly, we demonstrated two contrasting methods to deploy Cloud Run services – Terraform and the Google Cloud CLI.

In the next chapter, we will continue our journey by deploying a GKE architecture using only public Terraform modules.

8

Deploying GKE Using Public Modules

In *Chapter 4, Writing Reusable Code Using Modules*, we introduced modules and public registries. In this chapter, we will learn how to effectively use modules from the public Terraform Registry to build a complete architecture. We will see how we can deploy complex architectures quickly by utilizing public modules. In particular, we use two of the most popular Google Cloud modules from the Terraform Registry – the `network` and `kubernetes-engine` modules.

In this chapter, we will learn how to use modules from the public registry and use Terraform workspaces to provision two independent environments by doing the following:

- Developing a variable strategy
- Provisioning a network using a public Terraform module
- Provisioning a GKE cluster using a public Terraform module
- Using workspaces to provision deploy development and production environments

Technical requirements

In this chapter, we are provisioning a **Google Kubernetes Engine** (GKE) cluster. It helps to have a basic understanding of Kubernetes and GKE. We will deploy two independent GKE clusters in two different environments. We recommend using two projects for the two environments; however, you can also use a single project if you prefer. As in the previous two chapters, running Terraform in the cloud shell is easier, as we don't need to set up a Terraform service account and its IAM permission to provision the resources in both projects.

Please note that we will provision two GKE clusters with several VMs that incur costs. Depending on your quotas, you might not be able to have both GKE clusters running simultaneously in a single project.

After the exercise, it is important to destroy all the resources in both environments and access the web console to confirm that all VMs are removed.

The code for this chapter can be found here: `https://github.com/PacktPublishing/Terraform-for-Google-Cloud-Essential-Guide/tree/main/chap08`

Overview

As we mentioned in *Chapter 5*, *Managing Environments*, one of the fundamental principles in modern application development is maintaining **dev/prod parity** (`https://12factor.net/dev-prod-parity`). That is, different environments, such as development, testing, and production environments, should be as similar as possible. Terraform is the ideal tool to set up any number of environments and then delete them once they've been used. To minimize the cost, it is a common practice to provision smaller instance sizes or zonal resources instead of larger and regional resources in development environments. As we have discussed previously, by combining modules and workspaces, we can use Terraform to provision equivalent environments quickly and with minimal repeated effort.

In this exercise, we want to deploy two GKE clusters, one for development and one for production. The two clusters should be nearly identical, except that we want to save costs for the development cluster. Thus, we set up a regional high-availability cluster for production but a zonal cluster for development. In addition, we use small spot instances for the nodes in the development cluster but medium-sized regular instances for the production cluster. As the two environments are nearly identical, we use Terraform workspaces to manage the two environments.

Rather than starting from scratch, we utilize public modules. Both the Google blueprints and Terraform Registry contain many public modules. However, it's up to you to decide whether a public module actually adds value or whether you are better off with your own code.

For example, we already have very efficient code to enable the necessary Google Cloud APIs and provision a service account, so we use our previous code. Ideally, we would have stored the code in a private module repository, but for simplicity's sake, we will copy the code from the previous chapter.

Following Google's security guidelines, we will deploy the GKE cluster in a custom VPC. Looking through the modules, we decided on the following public modules:

- `network` (`https://registry.terraform.io/modules/terraform-google-modules/network/`) to build the custom VPC

- `kubernetes-engine` (`https://registry.terraform.io/modules/terraform-google-modules/kubernetes-engine`) to provision the actual GKE cluster

Developing a variable strategy

Our objective is to create GKE clusters for multiple independent environments. In our example, we provision two environments – development and production. However, we want to keep it flexible enough to provide additional environments, such as testing or staging, when required. We also want to balance flexibility with ease of use. For this, we need to decide on a variable strategy. First, we must determine which values might differ from environment to environment and which should remain the same regardless of the environment. For example, we know we want to have different values for the node pool configurations, such as the initial and maximum number of nodes, but cluster configuration attributes such as network policy and HTTP load balancing are the same regardless of the environment. Thus, we need to define variables for the node pools but not for cluster configurations.

Second, we must decide which variables to make optional and which ones should be required. The three main components that we want to parameterize are the network details, the node pool of the cluster, and the cluster itself, so we define each of these variables as an object to provide some type of constraint. In Terraform version 1.13, Hashicorp introduced default values to object types, which can be very useful. Thus, in our variable declaration, we make several variable declarations optional. For example, the name and the type of GKE cluster (zonal or region) and whether to use spot instances are required, whereas the machine type for the node pool, among other things, is optional. We follow a similar strategy for the network, and thus we declare the variables as follows:

chap08/variables.tf

```
variable "network" {
  type = object({
    name                 = string
    subnetwork_name      = string
    nodes_cidr_range     = optional(string, "10.128.0.0/20")
    pods_cidr_range      = optional(string, "10.4.0.0/14")
    services_cidr_range  = optional(string, "10.8.0.0/20")
  })
}
variable "gke" {
  type = object({
    name     = string
    regional = bool
    zones    = list(string)
  })
}
```

```
variable "node_pool" {
  type = object({
    name              = string
    machine_type      = optional(string, "e2-small")
    spot              = bool
    initial_node_count = optional(number, 2)
    max_count         = optional(number, 4)
    disk_size_gb      = optional(number, 10)
  })
}
```

Now that we have defined our variables, let's look at the public modules to provision the network and the GKE cluster.

Provisioning a network using the public module

Google maintains the Google Cloud Terraform network module (`https://registry.terraform.io/modules/terraform-google-modules/network/`). It is part of the Cloud Foundation Toolkit (`https://cloud.google.com/foundation-toolkit`), a set of Terraform modules that follow Google Cloud best practices.

The starting point for using any public module is documentation. A well-written module includes clear and concise documentation and examples for various use cases. For example, the `network` module contains sections for inputs, outputs, dependencies, resources used, and examples of common use cases. These examples are stored in a public GitHub repository so that we can examine them. Public modules are written to cater to many different requirements and can contain many variables and configurations. Thus, it's important to study the different configurations and input requirements. Furthermore, some modules have submodules that can be used independently. For example, the networking module contains **submodules** for subnets and firewall rules that you can use in your existing VPC network.

We are using the example in the `README` as a basis for our configuration. Our VPC runs the GKE cluster, so we want to define the secondary IP CIDR ranges for the pods and services. In addition, we might want to remotely log in to the nodes used for testing purposes using SSH but do so only via the IAP, so we add a firewall rule to the module.

The official Terraform registry supports module versioning, and it is good practice to use this feature and enforce version constraints. Modules published in the official registry must follow **semantic versioning** (`https://semver.org/`). That is, the version number follows the pattern of `major.minor.patch`. For example, `4.1.2` indicates major version 4, minor version 1, and patch level 2. When using public modules, it is recommended to use specific versions so that you control the updates. We are using version `5.2.0` for the `network` module.

In addition, this particular module has three required inputs: `project_id`, `network_name`, and a list of `subnets`. Looking at the documentation, the subnets are defined as a list of strings. Further down in the documentation, we see more details on the required and optional inputs for subnets.

While the main documentation clearly spells out the format for `subnets` and `secondary_ranges`, it only declares the firewall rules as any. In this case, we must go to the `submodules` documentation to determine the required inputs. The `submodules` documentation at `https://registry.terraform.io/modules/terraform-google-modules/network/google/latest/submodules/firewall-rules` gives a detailed list of the required and optional inputs for the firewall rules. With this in mind, we define our VPC module shown as follows:

chap08/vpc.tf

```
module "vpc" {
  source  = "terraform-google-modules/network/google"
  version = "= 5.2.0"
  depends_on = [google_project_service.this["compute"]]

  project_id   = var.project_id
  network_name = var.network.name

  subnets = [
    {
      subnet_name          = var.network.subnetwork_name
      subnet_ip            = var.network.nodes_cidr_range
      subnet_region        = var.region
      subnet_private_access = "true"
    },
  ]

  secondary_ranges = {
    (var.network.subnetwork_name) = [
      {
        range_name    = "${var.network.subnetwork_name}-pods"
        ip_cidr_range = var.network.pods_cidr_range
      },
```

```
        {
            range_name    = "${var.network.subnetwork_name}-
    services"
            ip_cidr_range = var.network.services_cidr_range
        },
    ]
}

    firewall_rules = [
      {
        name      = "${var.network.name}-allow-iap-ssh-ingress"
        direction = "INGRESS"
        ranges    = ["35.235.240.0/20"]
        allow = [{
          protocol = "tcp"
          ports    = ["22"]
        }]
      },
    ]
}
```

Now that we have defined the network, let's turn our attention to the provisioning of the GKE cluster.

Provisioning a GKE cluster using the public module

The Terraform kubernetes-engine module – https://registry.terraform.io/ modules/terraform-google-modules/kubernetes-engine/google/latest – is one of the more comprehensive (complex) Google Cloud Terraform modules. Our architecture calls for a zonal GKE cluster with a single configurable node pool for development and an equivalent but regional cluster for production. Thus, we start with the example in the README and modify it as per our needs. First, we remove features we don't require, such as node pool labels and metadata. Next, we parameterize several attributes that differ depending on the environment. This includes the network and the configuration of the nodes in the node pool. We also include a Boolean variable, which indicates whether the cluster is a zonal or a regional cluster.

Finally, we set several fixed attributes that remain constant regardless of the environment in which the cluster is deployed. One note regarding this module: it first creates a GKE cluster with a default node pool. Only after the cluster with the default node pool is generated does the module add the defined node pool. Thus, the last two attributes indicate the number of nodes in the initial, the default node pool, and whether to remove the default node pool. In our case, we don't care about the default node pool, so we set `initial_node_count` to 1 and `remove_default_node_pool` to true:

chap08/gke.tf

```
# google_client_config and kubernetes provider must be
# explicitly specified like the following.
data "google_client_config" "default" {
}
provider "kubernetes" {
  host                   = "https://${module.gke.endpoint}"
  token                  = data.google_client_config.default.
access_token
  cluster_ca_certificate = base64decode(module.gke.ca_
certificate)
}


locals {
  subnetwork_name = module.vpc.subnets["${var.region}/${var.
network.subnetwork_name}"].name
}


module "gke" {
  source     = "terraform-google-modules/kubernetes-engine/
google"
  version    = "23.1.0"
  project_id = var.project_id
  region     = var.region

  name     = var.gke.name
  regional = var.gke.regional
  zones    = var.gke.zones

  network           = module.vpc.network_name
  subnetwork        = local.subnetwork_name
  ip_range_pods     = "${local.subnetwork_name}-pods"
  ip_range_services = "${local.subnetwork_name}-services"
```

```
  service_account = google_service_account.this.email

  node_pools = [
    {
      name                   = var.node_pool.name
      machine_type           = var.node_pool.machine_type
      disk_size_gb           = var.node_pool.disk_size_gb
      spot                   = var.node_pool.spot
      initial_node_count     = var.node_pool.initial_node_count
      max_count              = var.node_pool.max_count
      disk_type              = "pd-ssd"
    },
  ]

  # Fixed values
  network_policy                = true
  horizontal_pod_autoscaling    = true
  http_load_balancing           = true
  create_service_account        = false

  initial_node_count            = 1
  remove_default_node_pool      = true
}
```

Now that we have defined the variable definitions and the modules, let's focus on the variable assignments.

Using workspaces to deploy to development and production environments

In *Chapter 5, Managing Environments*, we discussed the two main methods to support multiple environments using Terraform – workspaces and directory structure. In this case, we decide to use workspaces, as our two environments are very similar.

Thus, first, create two workspaces named dev and prod:

```
$ terraform workspace new prod
$ terraform workspace new dev
```

Once we have created the two workspaces, we write two variable definition files (.tfvars) for each of the two environments. Since we declared many of our variables as optional, the development variable definition file is quite short. It consists mainly of the zone in which we want to deploy the cluster and the names of the various cloud resources:

chap08/dev.tfvars

```
project_id = "<PROJECT_ID>"
region     = "us-west1"
zone       = "us-west1-a"

network = {
  name            = "dev-gke-network"
  subnetwork_name = "us-west1"
}

gke = {
  name  = "dev-gke-cluster"
  zones = ["us-west1-a"]
}

node_pool = {
  name = "dev-node-pool"
}

service_account = {
  name  = "dev-sa"
  roles = []
}
```

Now, we can deploy the development cluster by selecting the dev workspace, and running Terraform, specifying the appropriate .tfvars file shown as follows:

```
$ terraform workspace select dev
$ terraform apply -var-file=dev.tfvars
```

> **Note**
>
> Please note that this GKE module requires the Compute Engine API and the Kubernetes Engine API to be enabled before Terraform can run a Terraform plan. Hence, we included a small script to enable those APIs. Alternatively, we can enable them via the web console.

Creating a GKE cluster with a defined node pool does take some time. As mentioned, Terraform first creates a GKE cluster with a default node pool, and then creates a separately managed node pool. Thus, it can take up to 20 minutes for the cluster to be provisioned entirely. We can observe the nodes being created and deleted by using the console.

We include a sample file for the production cluster. Feel free to modify the file. We can deploy the production cluster in the same or a separate project. We need to update the project ID in the `prod.tfvars` file to deploy it into a separate project. If we use a service account rather than the cloud shell, we need to ensure that the service account has the right IAM permissions in both projects. We do not need to modify the backend location as Terraform writes the state file in the same bucket but under the appropriate workspace name.

To provision the production cluster, apply the equivalent commands for production:

```
$ terraform workspace select prod
$ terraform apply -var-file=prod.tfvars
```

Once the cluster is deployed, we can test it with any Kubernetes configurations. An interesting application is the **Online Boutique** sample application from Google at `https://github.com/GoogleCloudPlatform/microservices-demo`.

To use it, clone the repository, and connect to our GKE cluster using the `gcloud connect` command, before applying the configuration file shown as follows:

```
$ git clone https://github.com/GoogleCloudPlatform/
microservicesdemo.git
$ gcloud container clusters get-credentials dev-gke-cluster \
--zone us-west1-a --project <PROJECT_ID>
$ kubectl apply -f \
./microservices-demo/release/kubernetesmanifests.yaml
```

It takes a few minutes for the application to be fully deployed. Once it is, we can retrieve the public IP address using the following command and access it by using any browser:

```
$ kubectl get service frontend-external | awk '{print $4}'
```

If you get a 500 error in your browser, wait a few minutes, and reload it.

Summary

In this chapter, we learned how to utilize public modules. Public modules can help us create complex systems more rapidly than building them from scratch. Public modules are also an excellent resource for learning Terraform language tricks. All public modules reside in GitHub repositories and are free to explore.

Furthermore, we used workspaces to create two independent environments by writing two separate variable definition files and creating two workspaces. Creating a third environment is as easy as creating a new variable definitions file and workspace and running Terraform in that workspace. That is the power of Terraform.

Now that we have demonstrated different approaches to provision three very different architectures, we will introduce some tools to help us develop Terraform code more efficiently. Before we go on, be sure to delete the GKE clusters, as they incur considerable costs due to the number of VMs provisioned.

Part 3: Wrapping It Up: Integrating Terraform with Google Cloud

This part of the book shows how to combine Terraform with Google Cloud services and other tools to improve your workflow. As with any tool, Terraform works better in conjunction with other tools. In the next chapter, we introduce four third-party tools enabling you to develop and utilize Terraform code more efficiently than using it alone. We then conclude our journey by showing how you can integrate Terraform into your Google Cloud environment, and previewing a unique Google Cloud Terraform feature.

After reading this part of the book, you will have learned how to use Terraform with other tools and Google Cloud services to provide a better developer and user experience.

This part of the book comprises the following chapters:

- *Chapter 9, Developing Terraform Code Efficiently*
- *Chapter 10, Google Cloud Integration*

9

Developing Terraform Code Efficiently

Terraform's popularity and open source licensing model have spawned a very active ecosystem. Many open source and commercial tools and resources are available that extend its functionality and capabilities. An excellent resource is the curated list of Terraform resources at `https://github.com/shuaibiyy/awesome-terraform`. This chapter highlights four of the most common and practical tools to help you write and develop Terraform code more efficiently.

In this chapter, we cover the following topics:

- **Visual Studio Code (VS Code)** Terraform Extension
- `tflint`
- Checkov
- Terragrunt

Technical requirements

In this chapter, you need to install each of the tools discussed. We provide references on how to do so. The code for this chapter is at `https://github.com/PacktPublishing/Terraform-for-Google-Cloud-Essential-Guide/tree/main/chap09`.

VS Code Terraform Extension

> **Note**
> The code for this section is in the `chap09/vscode` directory in the GitHub repo of this book. However, in this section, you do not have to actually run Terraform.

VS Code is one of the most popular source code editors, and for a good reason. Managed and maintained by Microsoft, VS Code is open source and includes many features such as syntax highlighting and intelligent auto-completion. VS Code is extensible. At the time of writing this book, there are over 40,000 extensions available that add to the development workflow. One of them is the HashiCorp Terraform extension, which is managed and maintained by HashiCorp. If you already have VS Code on your local system, installing the HashiCorp Terraform extension is easy. Simply go to Visual Studio marketplace at `https://marketplace.visualstudio.com/items?itemName=HashiCorp.terraform` and hit the **Install** button.

Once installed, the extension is automatically activated in any folder or workspace that contains Terraform code. In this section, we will highlight the main features of the extension. One of the primary objectives of the Terraform extension is to keep you close to the code – that is, rather than exiting the editor to perform actions such as validation, formatting, or looking up definitions and declarations, the extension lets you perform those actions inside the editor, saving you time.

We are reusing the code from the *Writing flexible modules* section of *Chapter 4, Writing Reusable Code Using Modules*, to demonstrate some of the features.

Syntax highlighting and validation

Let's go ahead and open the `main.tf` and `./modules/main.tf` files, which we have slightly modified. We will see two features immediately. The first one is syntax highlighting. Terraform language constructs, such as modules, strings, and dynamic blocks, are color-coded for quick identification, making the code easier to read.

Second, the extension provides syntax validation. You may notice the unclosed configuration block in `main.tf` under the **Problems** tab (*Ctrl + Shift + M*). Syntax validation provides validation similar to `terraform validate` but without running the command explicitly. Go ahead and close the block by adding the missing } symbol, and the problem will disappear. Similarly, you can format the code without leaving the editor using the *Ctrl + Shitft + I* key combination. These features keep you close to the code, as you do not have to leave the editor:

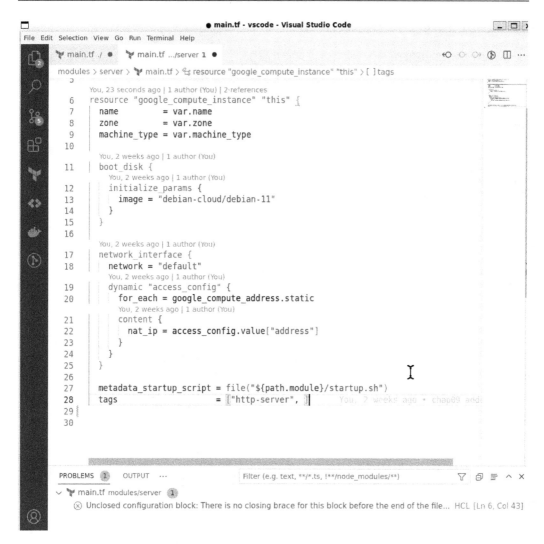

Figure 9.1 – Syntax highlighting and validation

Let's go to the **Terminal** tab and run `terraform init` to initialize Terraform in the current directory. While strictly not required, initializing Terraform will align with the provider version.

Intelligent auto-completion

Once we have initialized Terraform, we can see the true power of the Terraform extension. Let's start typing to declare a new resource – for example, `resource "google_compute_instance"`. As you type, the editor **autocompletes** your code – that is, the editor automatically provides the possible options for the text you have typed so far. As you provide more text, the choices narrow down to fewer options:

Figure 9.2 – Intelligent autocompletion

Staying with our example of `google_compute_resource`, once you decide from the list of options, the extension automatically fills in the required fields for that resource. Not only that but also if you hover the cursor over that block, the extension provides additional details for that block.

> **Note**
> For this feature, you must enable **Terraform | Experimental Features: Prefill Required Fields**.

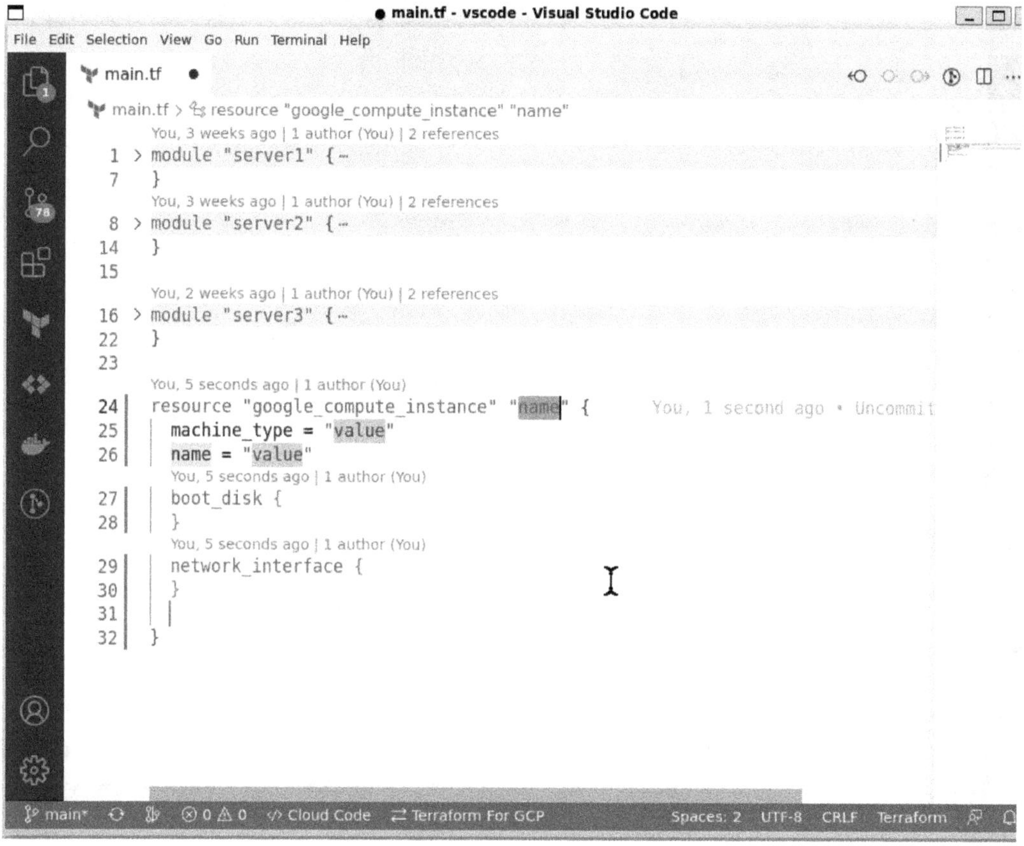

Figure 9.3 – Prefilling the required fields

Consistent in keeping you close to the code, the extension also provides easy code navigation.

Code navigation

To demonstrate this feature, let's open up the main.tf file and hover the cursor on var.zone on line 4. First, the extension tells us that this variable is of the string type. Right-clicking (or *Ctrl + Click* on Mac) brings up the context menu. This allows us to quickly go to the variable definition or see all the locations where the variable is referenced:

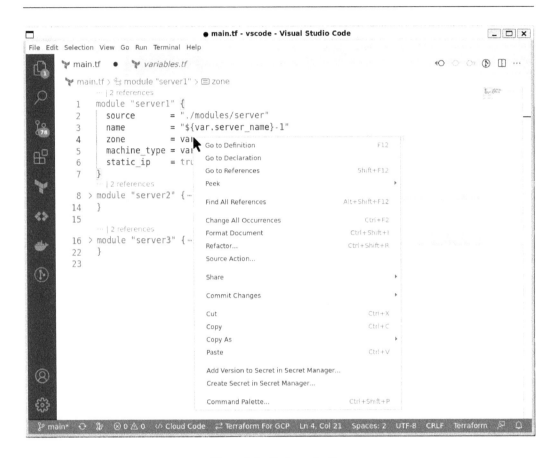

Figure 9.4 – Code navigation

This feature is useful when working with modules, and we want to investigate the code of the module. Let's bring the cursor to the value of the source definition of the module, for example, in line 2, and hit *F12* (go to **Definition**). We can peek at the definition, which gives us a view of the first few lines of the module code without switching over to the module file.

The VS Code Terraform extension is an excellent tool that increases productivity, and if you haven't done so, we highly recommend installing and using it.

tflint

In the Unix world, a **linter** is a static code analysis tool to detect minor errors. Initially created for the C programming language, many different lint programs have been developed, including for Terraform. Previously, we showed the `terraform validate` command, which validates your configuration, including the syntax and verification of reusable modules. This command is excellent for finding common syntax errors such as missing brackets or unclosed quotation marks. **tflint** (`https://`

github.com/terraform-linters/tflint) serves a similar function but detects possible errors, such as invalid instance types, and provides more information, such as any unused declaration, deprecated syntax, and violation of best practices. Therefore, tflint not only finds errors but also helps keep the code cleaner and easier to manage.

tflint consists of a single executable and extensible plugins. To install tflint on your machine, follow the instructions at https://github.com/terraform-linters/tflint#installation for your operating system. There is a default plugin for Terraform and plugins for different service providers, including Google Cloud.

To use the Google Cloud plugin, we define the plugins we want to use in a file called .tflint. hcl shown as follows:

chap09/tflint/.tflint.hcl

```
plugin "google" {
    enabled = true
    version = "0.21.0"
    source   = "github.com/terraform-linters/tflint-ruleset-
google"
}

plugin "terraform" {
  enabled = true
  preset   = "all"
}
```

After you have installed tflint and defined the plugins to be used, we need to initialize tflint. Once initialized, we can execute tflint to run it in the current directory:

```
$ tflint --init
$ tflint
```

We have included an example to show the type of errors and warnings that tflint reports. In this case, tflint reports the following:

- An **error**, as x2-micro is an invalid machine type
- A **warning** that the output, which is defined in main.tf, should be moved to output.tf to follow the best practices
- A **warning** that the static_ip variable is declared but not used
- A **notice** that the machine_type variable does not have a description

You can disable rules that you don't want `tflint` to report by setting the enabled flag to `false` in the `.tflint.hcl` file shown as follows:

chap09/tflint/.tflint.hcl

```
rule "terraform_documented_variables" {
  enabled = false
}
```

As you can see, `tflint` is a nice utility that helps you improve your workflow and write more consistent code. Hence, it is often used as one step in the CI/CD pipeline as we will show in the next chapter.

Checkov

Checkov is a static code analysis tool that checks for potential security and compliance issues. Its flexible design allows it to work with not only Terraform but also different kinds of IaC tools, including Docker and Helm. Checkov is implemented in Python and, similarly to `tflint`, uses rules called policies to check for potential security violations. As of the time of writing, over 150 Google Cloud-specific policies have been defined (`https://github.com/bridgecrewio/checkov/blob/master/docs/5.Policy%20Index/terraform.md`).

You can extend the predefined policies by creating custom policies using Python or YAML (`https://www.checkov.io/3.Custom%20Policies/Custom%20Policies%20Overview.html`).

Checkov is a complex tool with a multitude of options and extensions. Thus, we will only cover the basic functionality so you can decide whether to investigate it further.

As Checkov is implemented in Python, Python and `PIP` must be installed on your local system. You can find the installation instructions at `https://www.checkov.io/2.Basics/Installing%20Checkov.html`.

Once Checkov is installed, running it is straightforward:

```
$ checkov --directory .
```

We can see that the output provides a lot of information. It starts with the files scanned; the version information; and the number of passed, failed, and skipped checks. It then lists an entry for each checked rule. For each failed rule, Checkov lists the location in the file that violated the policy:

```
[ terraform framework ]: 100%|         |[3/3], Current File Scanned=variables.tf
[ secrets framework ]: 100%|         |[3/3], Current File Scanned=./main.tf


      __|  |_    ___  __|  |  __|  _ \ \ /
     / __| |   / _ \ / __| |  /  | (   )\ \ /
    | (__| __ <  __/| (__| < < (   ) \ v /
     \___|_| \_\\___|\___|_|\_\\_\___/ \_/


By bridgecrew.io | version: 2.2.38

terraform scan results:

Passed checks: 1, Failed checks: 1, Skipped checks: 1

Check: CKV_GCP_29: "Ensure that Cloud Storage buckets have uniform bucket-level access enabled"
        PASSED for resource: google_storage_bucket.this
        File: /main.tf:19-25
        Guide: https://docs.bridgecrew.io/docs/bc_gcp_gcs_2
Check: CKV_GCP_78: "Ensure Cloud storage has versioning enabled"
        FAILED for resource: google_storage_bucket.this
        File: /main.tf:19-25
        Guide: https://docs.bridgecrew.io/docs/ensure-gcp-cloud-storage-has-versioning-enabled

                19 | resource "google_storage_bucket" "this" {
                20 |   location                     = var.region
                21 |   name                         = "${var.project_id}-sample-bucket"
                22 |   uniform_bucket_level_access = true
                23 |
                24 |   #checkov:skip=CKV_GCP_62: "No loggin required"
                25 | }

Check: CKV_GCP_62: "Bucket should log access"
        SKIPPED for resource: google_storage_bucket.this
        Suppress comment:  "No loggin required"
        File: /main.tf:19-25
        Guide: https://docs.bridgecrew.io/docs/bc_gcp_logging_2
```

Figure 9.5 – Checkov output

The output for Checkov tends to be verbose and can quickly get overwhelming. We can use the `--quiet` and `--compact` flags to shorten the output. When the `--quiet` flag is set, Checkov only displays failed checks whereas the `--compact` flag does not display the code block.

Furthermore, there are times when we explicitly do not want to enforce certain rules. Checkov provides two mechanisms to skip rules. First, we can insert comments into the Terraform code to skip a rule and display an appropriate comment, such as `#checkov:skip=CKV_GCP_62: "No logging required"`.

Alternatively, we can specify the rules to skip using the `--skip-check` flag. Using the comment and the appropriate flag, the output now becomes more manageable:

```
$ checkov --directory . --skip-check CKV_GCP_78 \
--quiet --compact
```

```
terraform scan results:
Passed checks: 1, Failed checks: 0, Skipped checks: 1
```

In summary, `tflint` and Checkov are static code tools that you can incorporate into your workflow to make your Terraform code more maintainable and more secure.

Terragrunt

As you develop larger deployments, your Terraform code becomes more complex. You will also start to have teams working on the same deployment simultaneously. As discussed in previous chapters, it is advisable to break larger Terraform deployments into more manageable parts, each residing in its own subdirectory and each having its own state file. Unfortunately, that creates overhead, and you find yourself repeating yourself. For example, each subdirectory has its own `provider.tf` and `backend.tf` files. As we have already experienced, we cannot use interpolation in the `backend.tf` file and we need to edit each `backend.tf` file explicitly. Furthermore, we need to run Terraform in each subdirectory independently.

This is where **Terragrunt** comes into the picture. Terragrunt is defined as a *thin wrapper* to keep your Terraform code DRY – as in, in line with the **don't repeat yourself** (**DRY**) principle. Terragrunt achieves this by preparing each subdirectory, for example, by writing `backend.tf` files and then calling Terraform recursively. Thus, rather than individually preparing files in each subdirectory and then calling Terraform multiple times, we define Terragrunt configuration files and then call Terragrunt once in the root directory. Terragrunt performs all the necessary actions recursively, hence removing the need to repeat yourself.

The key features of Terragrunt are to define the backend and provider configurations once and to call Terraform with common CLI arguments recursively.

Let's see how to use Terragrunt in practice. To demonstrate the use, we will simulate a three-tier deployment similar to the one from *Chapter 6, Deploying a Traditional Three Tier Architecture*. We have a root directory with three subdirectories, `foundation`, `db`, and `main`. To speed things up, we will not provision any resources and will simply output values to demonstrate the flow.

Previously, we had to edit `backend.tf` explicitly to specify the bucket, and we also had to duplicate the `provider.tf` file. Furthermore, we then had to run Terraform in each subdirectory. While this overhead is manageable for this deployment, you can see how it may become cumbersome for more complex implementations and if deployed in multiple environments. With Terragrunt, we can reduce this overhead by creating several configuration files and deploying everything with a single command with no additional editing.

As before, the objective of this section is to give you a brief overview of the main features rather than a detailed description so you can decide whether Terragrunt suits your workflow.

To install Terragrunt, follow the instructions at `https://terragrunt.gruntwork.io/docs/getting-started/install/` for your operating system.

As Terraform, Terragrunt uses configuration files written in the HCL language, so we are familiar with the syntax. The configuration files are named `terragrunt.hcl` by default. We generally place one configuration file in the root directory for global directives and additional ones in each subdirectory. The `terragrunt.hcl` file in each subdirectory references (includes) the configuration files in the parent directories and adds some additional commands. Therefore, a typical directory structure using Terragrunt looks like the following:

```
├── db
│   ├── backend.tf
│   ├── main.tf
│   ├── output.tf
│   ├── provider.tf
│   ├── terragrunt.hcl
│   └── variables.tf
├── foundation
│   ├── backend.tf
│   ├── main.tf
│   ├── output.tf
│   ├── provider.tf
│   ├── terragrunt.hcl
│   └── variables.tf
├── main
│   ├── backend.tf
│   ├── main.tf
│   ├── output.tf
│   ├── provider.tf
│   ├── terragrunt.hcl
│   └── variables.tf
└── terragrunt.hcl
```

As mentioned, Terragrunt configuration files are written in the HCL syntax, so we start by defining some local variables used throughout the configuration file. To pass a variable value to Terragrunt, we can use an environment variable. This is especially useful to pass the Google project ID so that we don't have to define it or edit it in any file explicitly.

One of the most useful features of Terragrunt is to define the `remote_state` dynamically. As you have seen, a common practice is to store the same subdirectory structure for the remote state. Terragrunt provides several built-in functions that return paths relating to the directory structure. Therefore, we can define the remote state file generically for each subdirectory, shown as follows:

```
locals {
  project_id = get_env("GOOGLE_CLOUD_PROJECT")
```

```
   prefix      = "chap09/terragrunt"
 }
 remote_state {
   backend = "gcs"
   generate = {
     path      = "backend.tf"
     if_exists = "overwrite_terragrunt"
   }
   config = {
     bucket = "${local.project_id}-tf-state"
     prefix = "${local.prefix}/${path_relative_to_include()}/
 terraform.tfstate"
   }
 }
```

When we run Terragrunt, it dynamically generates a `backend.tf` file in the local subdirectory. First, it retrieves the value of the environment variable GOOGLE_CLOUD_PROJECT and assigns it to the local variable `project_id`. It then writes the `remote_state` block using the appropriate values for the bucket and prefix attribute. The prefix attribute will be `chap09/terragrunt/db` for the DB subdirectory and `chap09/terragrunt/main` for the main subdirectory.

The next block dynamically generates the `provider.tf` file, so that we do not have to repeat ourselves. The last block in the root `terragrunt.hcl` file defines the input variables to be passed to Terraform – that is, it serves the same purpose as the `terraform.tfvars` file, but again, we don't have to write the same file in each subdirectory:

```
generate "provider" {
   path      = "provider.tf"
   if_exists = "overwrite_terragrunt"
   contents  = <<EOF
provider "google" {
   project = local.project_id
   region  = var.region
   zone    = var.zone
}
EOF
}
```

```
# Indicate the input values to use for the variables of the
module.
inputs = {
  project_id = local.project_id
  region     = "us-west1"
  zone       = "us-west1-a"
}
```

Now that we have defined the configuration files in the root and the subdirectories, we can run Terragrunt recursively using the `terragrunt run-all` command:

$ terragrunt run-all init

The preceding command writes the `provider.tf` and `backend.tf` files in each subdirectory, and then runs `terraform init` in each subdirectory to initialize Terraform.

> **Note**
>
> Ensure that your GOOGLE_CLOUD_PROJECT environment variable is set, and if not, set it using the following command:
>
> ```
> GOOGLE_CLOUD_PROJECT=`gcloud info --format="value(config.
> project)"`
> ```

You may notice that Terragrunt has created two new files in each subdirectory: `provider.tf` and `backend.tf`. Looking into each `backend.tf` file, you see that the appropriate values for the bucket and prefix are filled in automatically.

Now, we can run Terraform recursively by calling `terragrunt run-all apply`. However, there is one more thing we need to do. By default, Terragrunt runs Terraform in parallel. In our case, this causes an error, as the different layers depend on each other. Remember that the `foundation` layer enables several APIs that the `db` layer requires, and the `main` layer requires the database to be in place. Thus, we need to instruct Terragrunt to run Terraform in sequence rather than in parallel. We do this by defining a **dependency** in the Terragrunt declaration file in each subdirectory:

chap09/terragrunt/db/terragrunt.hcl

```
include "root" {
  path = find_in_parent_folders()
}
```

```
dependencies {
  paths = ["../foundation"]
}
```

Therefore the Terragrunt configuration file in the database subdirectory contains two blocks. The `include` block references `terragrunt.hcl` of the root directory, and the `dependencies` block declares that Terraform can only be called in this directory after the `foundation` layer is complete.

With this in place, we can now run Terragrunt in the root directory using the following commands. Please note that `terragrunt apply` automatically adds an `-auto-approve` flag, so it is better to run the `plan` step explicitly:

```
$ terragrunt run-all plan
$ terragrunt run-all apply
```

Here, you can see how Terragrunt can help you to keep your Terraform code DRY. Previously, we had to edit several files each time we moved to a new project and then had to call Terraform multiple times. With Terragrunt, we can spare this work by defining the appropriate Terragrunt configuration files. However, please note that Terragrunt is not a panacea, and as with all other tools, we should apply it appropriately when it suits our workflow.

Summary

In this chapter, we introduced four commonly used tools in this chapter that can help you improve your Terraform workflow. We started with VSCode Terraform extension, which provides several intelligent capabilities to develop Terraform code more efficiently. We then showed two static code analysis tools. tflint helps you to catch specific errors before running Terraform, and it helps you to make your code more consistent. Checkov improves security by ensuring your Terraform conforms to a set of predefined and custom security policies. Lastly, Terragrunt can improve your efficiency by removing repetitive tasks.

These four tools only scratch the surface of the Terraform ecosystem. There are many more tools available, and more are developed every day. In our next and final chapter, we will see how to integrate Terraform into several Google Cloud services.

## 10

Google Cloud Integration

In this last chapter of our journey, we will take a look at how to integrate Terraform with specific Google Cloud services. In particular, we show how to use Cloud Build, Google Cloud's **Continuous Integration/Continuous Delivery (CI/CD)** service, to provision infrastructure using Terraform and build a service catalog that uses Terraform for its solution. We will then conclude with a feature of Google Cloud currently still in preview mode, which helps you import existing resources into Google Cloud but is also a great learning resource.

In this chapter, we will cover the following main topics:

- Using Terraform with Cloud Build
- Building a service catalog with Terraform solutions
- Importing and exporting Terraform resources

Technical requirements

This chapter has no special technical requirements, although general knowledge of CI/CD pipelines, and especially Cloud Build, is helpful. The code for this chapter is at `https://github.com/PacktPublishing/Terraform-for-Google-Cloud-Essential-Guide/tree/main/chap10`.

Using Terraform with Cloud Build

> **Note**
> The code for this section is under the `chap10/cloudbuild` directory in the GitHub repository of this book.

Cloud Build is Google Cloud's CI/CD platform. It is considered to be a serverless service, as we don't have to provision or manage any servers to utilize it. This makes it an ideal platform to run Terraform, particularly as you grow your team and your deployments become more complex.

To start using Cloud Build, you must first configure it by enabling the Cloud Build API and setting the appropriate service account permission. Cloud Build uses a Google Cloud service account with an email address of `<PROJECT-NUMBER>@cloudbuild.gserviceaccount.com`. We can enable the necessary IAM permission at `https://console.cloud.google.com/cloud-build/settings/service-account`, or if we require additional IAM roles, we can set them in the **IAM** section. For our example, we only need the **Compute Engine** permission, as shown in *Figure 10.1*:

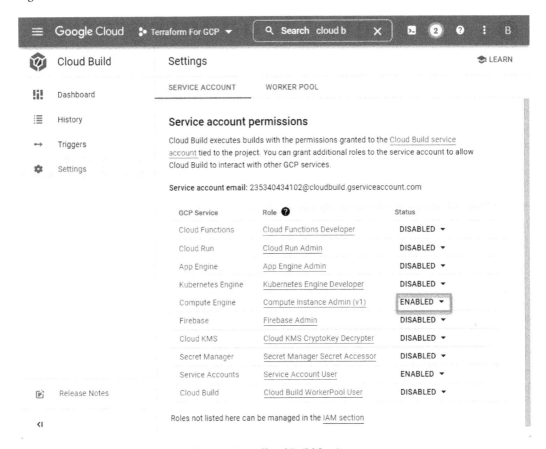

Figure 10.1 – Cloud Build Settings

We define the steps for Cloud Build in a configuration file. The basic workflow of Terraform in a CI/CD workflow is the same as it is on the CLI with some minor adjustments to ensure a smooth flow. First, we explicitly run the Terraform `plan` step and save the plan in a file. Second, we run `apply` for Terraform using the saved `plan` file as an argument. The primary reason for separating the `plan` and `apply` steps is so that Cloud Build terminates if the plan has any errors and does not attempt the final `apply` step. We also attach the `-auto-approve` flag to skip the interactive approval step, and add the `-input=false` flag so that Terraform does not ask for any input of variables that are not set. We can also include a check of `tflint` and abort the pipeline if it doesn't pass.

Thus, our workflow is as follows:

```
$ terraform init -input=false
$ tflint --init
$ tflint
$ terraform plan -input=false -out=tfplan
$ terraform apply -auto-approve -input=false tfplan
```

Cloud Build uses a configuration file that provides the instructions for the pipeline (https://cloud. google.com/build/docs/overview#build_configuration_and_build_steps). The configuration file format is either YAML or JSON, but we generally use YAML format, as it is easier to edit. A configuration file consists of a number of build steps executed in sequence. Each build step has several fields that define the details of the step. Cloud Build uses **Docker** under the hood, so we specify the Docker image to be pulled using the name field and specify the arguments passed to the Docker container using the args field. We can pass parameters in our configurations using the substitution block. For example, we can pass the Terraform version as an argument to Cloud Build with a default value or on the command line. Thus, our basic Cloud Build configuration is shown as follows:

chap10/cloudbuild/cloudbuild.yaml

```
steps:
- id: 'terraform init'
  name: 'hashicorp/terraform:${_TERRAFORM_VERSION}'
  args:
  - 'init'
  - '-input=false'

- id: 'tflint init'
  name: 'ghcr.io/terraform-linters/tflint-bundle'
  args:
  - '--init'

- id: 'tflint'
  name: 'ghcr.io/terraform-linters/tflint-bundle'
- id: 'terraform plan'
  name: 'hashicorp/terraform:${_TERRAFORM_VERSION}'
  args:
  - 'plan'
```

```
      - '-input=false'
      - '-out=tfplan'

   - id: 'terraform apply'
     name: 'hashicorp/terraform:${_TERRAFORM_VERSION}'
     args:
      - 'apply'
      - '-auto-approve'
      - '-input=false'
      - 'tfplan'

  substitutions:
    _TERRAFORM_VERSION: 1.3.0
```

Once we have defined the `cloudbuild.yaml` file, we can now run `cloudbuild` directly from the command line as follows:

```
$ gcloud builds submit
```

Cloud Build creates a temporary tarball which is a **tar** archive file of the current directory, uploads it into Cloud Storage, and then executes the build steps as defined in the configuration file. We can observe the progress on the command line, but a better way to see the details is to check under the **History** tab of the Cloud Build console as shown in *Figure 10.2*. If we click on the **Build** ID, we see the details of each step and what, if anything, went wrong. For example, we can change the machine type in `terraform.tfvars` to an incorrect value and rerun the build. We see that `tflint` catches the error and does not proceed to the `plan` and `apply` steps:

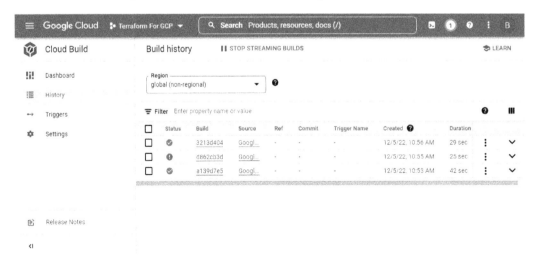

Figure 10.2 – Cloud Build console

> **Note**
>
> To reduce the size of the tarball, we can specify the files to be excluded in the `.gcloudignore` file, which is similar to a `.gitignore` file.

To make Cloud Build a truly continuous CI/CD pipeline, that is, to start a build process automatically rather than calling it from the CLI, we need to set up a trigger. A trigger automatically starts a build as soon as we check our code into a source code repository. To know more details to set up a trigger and link to different source code systems, such as GitHub or BitBucket, refer to the documentation at `https://cloud.google.com/build/docs/triggers`.

Building a service catalog with Terraform solutions

> **Note**
>
> A Google Cloud organization is required to create a service catalog. See *Creating and managing organizations* (`https://cloud.google.com/resource-manager/docs/creating-managing-organization`) for how to create an organization.

A service catalog enables IT organizations to offer approved services to an enterprise. Google Cloud provides a service catalog as a managed service to offer cloud services using a self-service model, which is one of the essential characteristics of cloud computing (`https://bigdatawg.nist.gov/_uploadfiles/M0006_v1_3333767255.pdf`).

That is, a user can browse a service catalog, pick from a list of service offerings, and then provision the required resources. Behind the scenes, we use Terraform to provision the solution, so the end user does not need to know the details of Terraform and uses an easy-to-use web interface to fill out any configuration details. The service catalog solution hides the complexity and ensures that the solution adheres to security and compliance policies. For example, *Figure 10.3* shows an example of a service catalog that lets users provision a server using different operating systems.

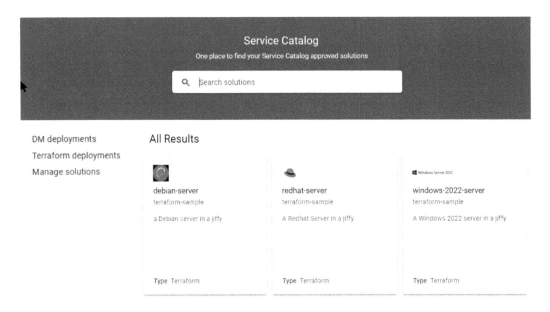

Figure 10.3 – Service Catalog

After selecting the solution, the user fills in the configuration details for the particular solution, as shown in *Figure 10.4*, and clicks on the **Preview and Deploy** button to deploy the solution:

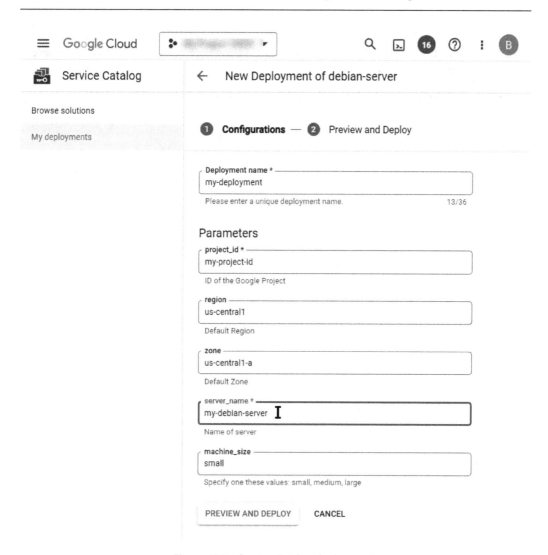

Figure 10.4 – Service Catalog deployment

We use the **Service Catalog Admin** console to define a service catalog and assign the solutions to be offered in the service catalog. We first create the appropriate Terraform configuration files to add a Terraform solution. The configuration should not define a remote backend or variable definitions. That is, it should not include `backend.tf` or `terraform.tfvars` files. The service catalog manages the remote backends for each actual deployment. As shown in *Figure 10.4*, all the declared variables are presented as parameters to fill in when the solution is given to the user, so we should include a good description and default value for each variable. This is where variable mapping, as introduced in *Chapter 4, Writing Reusable Code Using Modules*, comes in handy, as it can hide some of the complexity from the end user. For example, the user will likely only care about the general size of the machine instead of the actual machine type.

Once, we have defined the Terraform configuration, we need to combine all the files into a single zip file, and upload it to a Google Cloud Storage bucket. Please note that this bucket needs to have versioning enabled.

Once the Terraform config is uploaded, we can add the solution, as shown in *Figure 10.5*:

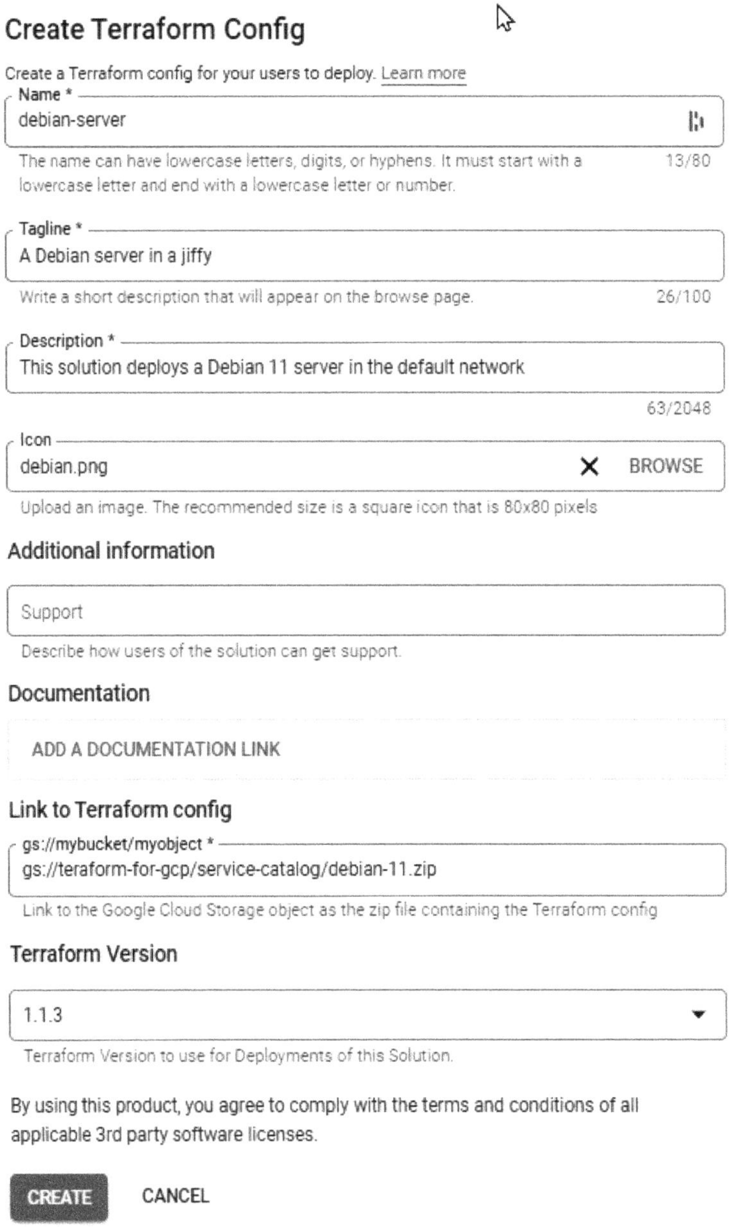

Create Terraform Config

Create a Terraform config for your users to deploy. Learn more

Name *
debian-server   13/80

The name can have lowercase letters, digits, or hyphens. It must start with a lowercase letter and end with a lowercase letter or number.

Tagline *
A Debian server in a jiffy   26/100

Write a short description that will appear on the browse page.

Description *
This solution deploys a Debian 11 server in the default network   63/2048

Icon
debian.png   ✕   BROWSE

Upload an image. The recommended size is a square icon that is 80x80 pixels

Additional information

Support

Describe how users of the solution can get support.

Documentation

ADD A DOCUMENTATION LINK

Link to Terraform config

gs://mybucket/myobject *
gs://teraform-for-gcp/service-catalog/debian-11.zip

Link to the Google Cloud Storage object as the zip file containing the Terraform config

Terraform Version

1.1.3   ▼

Terraform Version to use for Deployments of this Solution.

By using this product, you agree to comply with the terms and conditions of all applicable 3rd party software licenses.

CREATE   CANCEL

Figure 10.5 – Terraform solution

The service catalog uses Cloud Build to execute service catalog deployments. It handles all the details, such as constructing the Cloud Build configuration files and managing the states for the actual deployments. You can share a service catalog across multiple projects within (or even outside of) your organization. Users can then easily deploy solutions provided by a Terraform configuration. They also can change the deployment by changing the machine size, or they can destroy the deployment.

Importing and exporting Terraform resources

> **Note**
>
> The code for this section is under the `chap10/import-export` directory in the GitHub repository of this book. We recommend that you create a new project for this exercise.

In *Chapter 2, Exploring Terraform*, we discussed the concept of configuration drift: changes made outside of Terraform. Once we start using Terraform, we should not use the web console or `gcloud` to manage cloud inafrastructure resources. However, what do we do when there is an existing cloud resource we want to manage using Terraform?

Terraform provides the capability to import existing infrastructure resources. What this means is that we can bring existing resources into the realm of Terraform by using the command `terraform import` (learn more about it from here – `https://developer.hashicorp.com/terraform/cli/import`). However, this is often easier said than done. We should resort to importing existing resources only as a last option because bringing an existing cloud resource into the realm of your Terraform configuration is essentially a reverse engineering process. `terraform import` is only the first step of this process.

Let us demonstrate this. For this exercise, we start with a fresh Google Cloud project. First, we create a virtual machine through the web console or `gcloud`, shown as follows:

```
$ gcloud services enable cloudasset.googleapis.com
$ gcloud compute instances create myinstance  \
--zone=us-central1-a
```

Now, if we look at the Terraform state file, it is empty, as we created this virtual machine outside of Terraform.

To import an existing resource, we need two items. First, we must create a skeleton resource definition of the item we want to import. In our case, this is a `google_compute_instance`. Thus, we need to create a file shown as follows:

chap10/import-export/import.tf

```
resource "google_compute_instance" "myinstance" {
}
```

Second, we need to know the ID of the resource to be imported. In our case, we want the ID of the compute instance named `myinstance`. In Google Cloud, the syntax of IDs varies from cloud resource to resource. The specifics of the format can be found at `https://cloud.google.com/iam/docs/full-resource-names`. For a compute engine, the full resource name is `//compute.googleapis.com/projects/project-id/zones/zone/instances/instance-id`, so we can import the virtual machine with the following command:

```
$ terraform init
$ terraform import google_compute_instance.myinstance \
//compute.googleapis.com/projects/<PROJECT-ID>/zones/
us-central1-a/instances/myinstance
```

Now, the virtual machine is in the state file and hence in the realm of Terraform. Therefore, if we run `terraform state list`, we can see the resource.

However, we do not have a usable configuration file. If we run `terraform plan`, we get a number of error messages because the configuration file for `myinstance` is incomplete. This is where the reverse engineering process starts. We need to fill in all the required attributes and ensure they are consistent with the state file. This often becomes an iterative process – fill in attributes, run `terraform plan`, and repeat the process until Terraform reports no errors and detects no changes. At this point, the configuration file is consistent with our current state file. This process is tedious, particularly when we want to import multiple resources.

Google Cloud export

Google Cloud introduced a new feature that lets you export Google Cloud resources directly in the Terraform format. You can learn about this more here – `https://cloud.google.com/docs/terraform/resource-management/export`.

> **Note**
>
> As of writing this chapter (November 2022), this feature was only available in *preview*, meaning it can change without any notice.

To start using the feature, we need to enable the `cloudasset` API and install the Config Connector CLI:

```
$ gcloud services enable cloudasset.googleapis.com
$ gcloud components install config-connector
```

This feature is useful in more ways than one. First, by exporting a resource into the Terraform format, it creates a ready-to-use Terraform configuration file. Thus, we can create a compliant Terraform configuration by running the following command:

```
$ gcloud beta resource-config bulk-export \
    --resource-types=ComputeInstance \
    --project=<PROJECT-ID>  \
    --resource-format=terraform > import.tf
```

When we run `terraform plan`, Terraform reports no errors and no changes. However, once we have a look at the `input.tf` file, we see that the configuration is not quite ready to use. Many of the values in the configuration file are fully qualified resource names. Furthermore, if we run `terraform destroy` and `terraform plan` again, Terraform reports several errors. Thus, edits are still required before the configuration file becomes truly usable. For example, we want to remove any spurious attributes and replace many fully qualified values with variables.

Therefore, the Google Cloud export feature is useful when for bringing resources into the realm of Terraform. However, this feature is handy in another way. Terraform syntax can sometimes be confusing, especially when you are new to Terraform. While the documentation is good and often includes examples, it cannot show all variations. However, with the export feature, we can generate our own examples. We can create a cloud resource using the web console and then generate a fully compliant Terraform configuration file. The web console is easy to use, as all the options and features are clearly labeled.

For example, let's say we want to create a storage bucket with versioning but are unsure of the exact syntax of the Terraform configuration, so we create a storage bucket using the web console. We set the maximum number of versions per object to 5, and the expiration of non-current versions to 30 days, as shown in *Figure 10.6*:

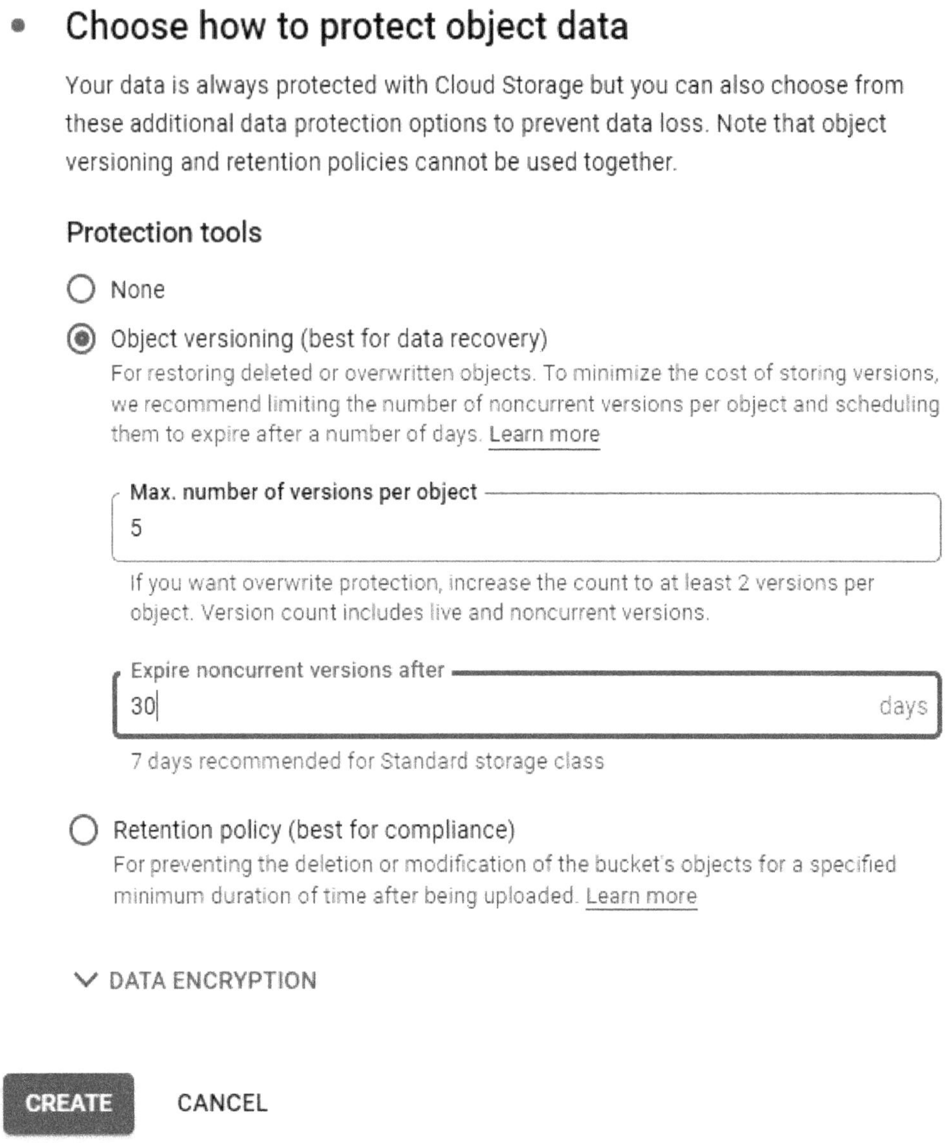

● Choose how to protect object data

Your data is always protected with Cloud Storage but you can also choose from these additional data protection options to prevent data loss. Note that object versioning and retention policies cannot be used together.

Protection tools

○ None

◉ Object versioning (best for data recovery)
For restoring deleted or overwritten objects. To minimize the cost of storing versions, we recommend limiting the number of noncurrent versions per object and scheduling them to expire after a number of days. Learn more

> Max. number of versions per object
>
> 5

If you want overwrite protection, increase the count to at least 2 versions per object. Version count includes live and noncurrent versions.

> Expire noncurrent versions after
>
> 30   days

7 days recommended for Standard storage class

○ Retention policy (best for compliance)
For preventing the deletion or modification of the bucket's objects for a specified minimum duration of time after being uploaded. Learn more

∨ DATA ENCRYPTION

CREATE   CANCEL

Figure 10.6 – Cloud Storage Bucket with versioning

We can then create the Terraform configuration file shown as follows to create an example of a compliant configuration:

```
$ gcloud beta resource-config bulk-export \
   --resource-types=StorageBucket \
   --project=<PROJECT_ID>  \
   --resource-format=terraform > bucket.tf
```

The file still requires some editing, but we now have an excellent example of how to create a bucket with versioning enabled, specify the maximum number of versions, and expire noncurrent versions.

This feature can also reveal some interesting aspects of Google Cloud. For example, you can provision a GKE cluster only using the default values and then export all resources in that project:

```
$ gcloud container clusters create-auto mycluster \
--region=us-central1
$ gcloud beta resource-config bulk-export \
--path=gkeout --project=<PROJECT_ID> \
--resource-format=terraform
```

We can see a large number of Terraform files in various subdirectories. This reveals all the cloud resources that are created behind the scenes. For example, we can see the default node pool configuration and several GKE-specific firewall rules.

Please note that at the time of writing, the export feature does not support all Google Cloud resource types, but we hope that when this feature becomes generally available, most resource types will be supported.

So far, we have seen that, while technically possible, importing existing resources is an exercise of reverse engineering and should only be used as a last resort, particularly for multiple and complex resources. The unique Google Cloud export feature can help in this process, but the feature is actually more helpful as a learning resource.

Summary

The final chapter covered how to integrate Terraform into Google Cloud services. Cloud Build is Google Cloud's CI/CD service and a great way to incorporate Terraform into a CI/CD pipeline. Service Catalog enables IT organizations to offer solutions built by Terraform to the enterprise while managing the distribution and ensuring compliance with internal security and compliance policies.

Lastly, we showed an interesting preview feature of Google Cloud to export existing resources directly into Terraform. This feature can be used to bring existing cloud resources under the control of Terraform as an absolute last resource. However, it can very useful as a learning tool.

Closing thoughts

Congratulations on making it to the end of this book! We hope you enjoyed the journey as much as we did guiding you. There is a reason Terraform is by far the most popular IAC tool. Terraform is powerful, yet it is easy to get started with. The workflow is straightforward, and the syntax is easy to understand. However, as is the case with any other tool, it takes time and experience to master Terraform. We encourage you to experiment. The beauty of Terraform is that it is as easy and fast to destroy cloud resources as it is to create them. Learn from others. Review the code of the modules in the Terraform Registry and the Google Terraform blueprints.

While each cloud provider has its own unique set of resources, the techniques and best practices are similar regardless of the provider, so study the best practices and apply what works for you.

The Terraform ecosystem is vibrant. New tools, both commercial and open source, appear all the time. Some of them are valuable, others not as much.

Lastly, consider getting certified. The Hashicorp Terraform Associate certification is a badge of honor and proves your proficiency in Terraform. The exam is provider-agnostic, and we have covered most of the topics included in the exam. We are confident that with a little bit of additional preparation, you will pass the exam and become a certified Terraform Associate.

And never stop learning!

Index

Packt.com

Subscribe to our online digital library for full access to over 7,000 books and videos, as well as industry leading tools to help you plan your personal development and advance your career. For more information, please visit our website.

Why subscribe?

- Spend less time learning and more time coding with practical eBooks and Videos from over 4,000 industry professionals

- Improve your learning with Skill Plans built especially for you

- Get a free eBook or video every month

- Fully searchable for easy access to vital information

- Copy and paste, print, and bookmark content

Did you know that Packt offers eBook versions of every book published, with PDF and ePub files available? You can upgrade to the eBook version at packt.com and as a print book customer, you are entitled to a discount on the eBook copy. Get in touch with us at customercare@packtpub.com for more details.

At www.packt.com, you can also read a collection of free technical articles, sign up for a range of free newsletters, and receive exclusive discounts and offers on Packt books and eBooks.

Other Books You May Enjoy

If you enjoyed this book, you may be interested in these other books by Packt:

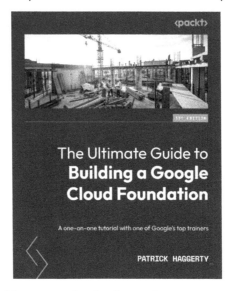

The Ultimate Guide to Building a Google Cloud Foundation

Patrick Haggerty

ISBN: 978-1-80324-085-5

- Create an organizational resource hierarchy in Google Cloud
- Configure user access, permissions, and key Google Cloud Platform (GCP) security groups
- Construct well thought out, scalable, and secure virtual networks
- Stay informed about the latest logging and monitoring best practices
- Leverage Terraform infrastructure as code automation to eliminate toil
- Limit access with IAM policy bindings and organizational policies
- Implement Google's secure foundation blueprint

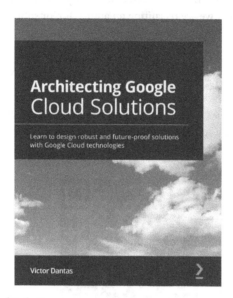

Architecting Google Cloud Solutions

Victor Dantas

ISBN: 978-1-80056-330-8

- Get to grips with compute, storage, networking, data analytics, and pricing
- Discover delivery models such as IaaS, PaaS, and SaaS
- Explore the underlying technologies and economics of cloud computing
- Design for scalability, business continuity, observability, and resiliency
- Secure Google Cloud solutions and ensure compliance
- Understand operational best practices and learn how to architect a monitoring solution
- Gain insights into modern application design with Google Cloud
- Leverage big data, machine learning, and AI with Google Cloud

Packt is searching for authors like you

If you're interested in becoming an author for Packt, please visit `authors.packtpub.com` and apply today. We have worked with thousands of developers and tech professionals, just like you, to help them share their insight with the global tech community. You can make a general application, apply for a specific hot topic that we are recruiting an author for, or submit your own idea.

Share Your Thoughts

Now you've finished *Terraform for Google Cloud Essential Guide*, we'd love to hear your thoughts! Scan the QR code below to go straight to the Amazon review page for this book and share your feedback or leave a review on the site that you purchased it from.

`https://packt.link/r/1804619620`

Your review is important to us and the tech community and will help us make sure we're delivering excellent quality content.

Download a free PDF copy of this book

Thanks for purchasing this book!

Do you like to read on the go but are unable to carry your print books everywhere? Is your eBook purchase not compatible with the device of your choice?

Don't worry, now with every Packt book you get a DRM-free PDF version of that book at no cost.

Read anywhere, any place, on any device. Search, copy, and paste code from your favorite technical books directly into your application.

The perks don't stop there, you can get exclusive access to discounts, newsletters, and great free content in your inbox daily

Follow these simple steps to get the benefits:

1. Scan the QR code or visit the link below

https://packt.link/free-ebook/9781804619629

2. Submit your proof of purchase
3. That's it! We'll send your free PDF and other benefits to your email directly

www.ingramcontent.com/pod-product-compliance
Lightning Source LLC
Chambersburg PA
CBHW060135060326
40690CB00018B/3885